COMPUTERS
—AND—
EFFECTIVE
INSTRUCTION

Using Computers and Software
in the Classroom

COMPUTERS
AND
EFFECTIVE INSTRUCTION

Using Computers and Software in the Classroom

David L. Lillie
Wallace H. Hannum
Gary B. Stuck

University of North Carolina—Chapel Hill

Longman

New York & London

Computers and Effective Instruction

Longman Inc., 95 Church Street, White Plains, N.Y. 10601

Associated companies:
Longman Group Ltd., London
Longman Cheshire Pty., Melbourne
Longman Paul Pty., Auckland
Copp Clark Pitman, Toronto
Pitman Publishing Inc., New York

Executive editor: Ray O'Connell
Development editor: Virginia L. Blanford
Production editor: Carol Harwood
Text design: Jill Francis Wood
Cover design: Susan J. Moore
Cover photo: National Education Association/Joe Di Dio
Text art: Charlene Felker and Hal Keith
Production supervisor: Kathleen M. Ryan

Library of Congress Cataloging-in-Publication Data
Lillie, David L.
    Computers and effective instruction.

    Bibliography: p.
    Includes index.
    1. Computer-assisted instruction—United States.
I. Hannum, Wallace H. II. Stuck, Gary B. III. Title.
LB1028.5.L497 1989   371.3'9445   88-23077
ISBN 0-8013-0003-7

88 89 90 91 92 93 94 9 8 7 6 5 4 3 2 1

Contents

Preface

The purpose of this text is to develop a bridge between what we know about effective instructional procedures and the use of computers for instruction in the public schools. In building such a bridge, the concepts and principles about the use of computers as tools for instruction presented in this text are based on a foundation of effective teaching and instructional design research. We believe that the effective use of computers as an instructional medium requires instructionally sound procedures. In this respect, we have emphasized the use of computers as a tool to facilitate and support effective instruction.

Unlike many textbooks addressing the role of computers in education, this book does not focus on descriptions of computer hardware and educational software. We assume that most teachers and students reading this text will have had initial exposure to computers, through their own personal or educational experiences or through an introductory workshop or course. Basic information *about* computers, such as the type or the make, computer capacities, ease of use, and cost, are topics coincidental to the main theme of the text—using computers to support the teaching and learning process. Improvements in the use of computers for instruction depend more on our knowledge and understanding of the advances in instructional technology than on the advances in computer technology. Information about specific instructional applications are presented to provide concrete examples of principles and procedures.

Educators involved in using computers for instruction must base decisions on information and knowledge that go beyond the "computer literacy'' level. For effective instruction to take place, practicing professionals must have the ability to use computers effectively within the discipline of education. It is our belief that for the remainder of this century, the use of computers in schools will occur in human-oriented, teacher-directed learning environments. Within the context of the total school curriculum, informed educators should be able to make decisions about when computers should be used, for what purposes, and with what software applications. Strengths and weaknesses of a proposed instructional application should be considered within the context of what we know about instructional models that work, documented instructional procedures, and the time-tested principles of instructional design.

Chapter 1 organizes and presents the concepts, principles, and procedures that are involved in the use of computers for instruction. Chapter 2 provides a foundation for the remainder of the book, by presenting the principles derived from what we know about effective instruction. This discussion of effective instruction is presented in the context of instructional uses of computers. Chapter 3 presents concepts and principles of instructional design that are important for the effective use of computers. The chapter provides guidelines for the selection of software programs and their integration into the curriculum. Chapter 4 addresses the first stage of instruction—establishing instructional objectives and developing instructional plans. This chapter discusses curricular scope and sequence, instructional objectives, and other concepts embedded in the mastery learning approach to instruction. Computer-based procedures available to manage instructional objectives and objective mastery at the classroom level are also presented.

Perhaps one of the greatest uses of computers in education today is in the area of assessment and evaluation. Computers are used to facilitate test administration, test scoring, and test analysis. Methods and procedures involving assessment activities and computers are presented in chapter 5. Chapter 6 addresses the use of computers for the instruction of special education students. Topics in this chapter include special applications, such as speech synthesizers for sight impaired and multihandicapped students as well as special software applications for other students with special learning problems. Chapter 7 presents methods and procedures to evaluate and select appropriate instructional software. The final chapter, chapter 8, discusses what to expect in the coming years, with the computer as a tool for effective and creative instruction.

Educational research has provided the profession of education with a solid foundation of information about effective instructional procedures and the effective design of materials developed to instruct. This rich reservoir of knowledge provides us with a base for applying computers to the task of instruction. The extent to which we will see dramatic changes in public school instruction stimulated by the informed use of computer technology depends on all of us: teachers, school administrators, teacher trainers, and educational policy makers.

D.L.L.
W.H.H.
G.B.S.

COMPUTERS
AND
EFFECTIVE
INSTRUCTION

Using Computers and Software
in the Classroom

CHAPTER 1

Computers and the Instructional Process

Objectives

After reading this chapter, you should be able to do the following:

1. Describe the educational goals that some educators believe will be more easily achieved with the use of computers.
2. List and describe the three levels of computer competency and explain why educators should seek to attain at least the first two.
3. List and discuss the major assumptions about the use of computers for instruction that underlie this book.
4. Describe the instructional model that is used as a conceptual framework for this book.
5. Define computer-managed instruction and provide a rationale for its use.

INTRODUCTION: THE INTEGRATION OF COMPUTERS IN THE SCHOOLS

There is no question that the use of computer technology in the nation's elementary and secondary schools, as well as colleges and universities, is increasing dramatically. In 1978, half of all U.S. high schools had no computers at all. In 1985, the typical high school had more than twenty computers, and the typical elementary school six. In many high schools today, a student can use computers to write compositions; to study content, facts, and knowledge; to understand relationships and concepts in mathematics and science; and to write computer programs—using computers for as much as an hour or two per day. During 1986, over 50% of the elementary and middle school pupils in the United States made some use of computers at school, even though many of these uses were casual and of short duration. By far the most revealing statistic on computer use in the schools is that the amount of time the average elementary school student spent on computers actually doubled from 1983 to 1985 (Becker, 1987).

Our nation's schools and educators have clearly hopped on the computer bandwagon. The real question is, are we just along for the ride or are we in control of where we are going? As with many fast developing trends in education, the actual use of computers in the schools for instructional purposes has outdistanced the development of concepts, theories, principles, and procedures that provide the foundation for appropriate applications.

To keep pace with the increasing use of computers, school systems and teacher training programs across the country have initiated an array of new computer-technology training efforts. Teacher training programs now include a variety of noteworthy introductory computer courses. For the most part, these courses focus on how computers work, how to select appropriate software and hardware (usually from the viewpoint of technology), and how to use some well-known applications packages. They also deal to some extent with the issues raised in using computers in the schools. Occasionally, courses include an introduction to a programming language.

The phrase coined to refer to the expected result of these courses is *computer literacy*. What specific competencies are included under this term depends on which of the many definitions you happen to be using. In fact, there are about as many definitions for computer literacy as there are books on the subject of computers in education. In general, however, computer literacy refers to a basic level of knowledge and skill in using a computer.

COMPUTER COMPETENCY FOR EDUCATORS

Ellen and Michael Vasu (1987) have developed a three-level framework for thinking about the knowledge and skills needed in using computers. Although their focus is on the integration of computers into the social science curricula of higher education, their framework also works well for the field of education. Within this framework, basic *computer literacy* is defined as a basic knowledge of the structure of computer systems—hardware and software. All professionals, they suggest, should possess this basic knowedge. With the increasing use of computers in homes, schools, and society in general, of course, more and more educators (as well as students) come to the classroom already computer literate. Consequently, the need to acquaint educators with how to operate personal computers is diminishing. The challenge that remains, however, is the development of knowledge and understanding about why, when, and how computers can be used to support effective instruction. Using computers as tools for improving the effectiveness of instruction in our schools hinges on the capacity of teachers and administrators to make informed curriculum decisions—decisions that are grounded in knowledge about effective instruction as well as about computers.

As illustrated in Table 1.1, a second level of computer knowledge, called *instructional applications,* is built on a foundation of basic computer literacy. This second level requires competency in computer

TABLE 1.1. COMPUTER LITERACY LEVELS FOR EDUCATORS

	Skills/Competencies
Level I Basic knowledge	Understanding of basic computer jargon (i.e., disk drive, CPU, menu-driven, control keys, memory, save, retrieve, etc.)
	Ability to use basic application programs (i.e., word processing, courseware, etc.)
	Elementary understanding of basic hardware components
Level II Instructional applications	All of the above plus
	Ability to select and match software with instructional objectives and individual needs of students
	Ability to evaluate courseware in terms of effective instruction and instructional design principles
	Application skills in using courseware, instructional management software, and test-scoring software
	Ability to match design of courseware to individual instructional needs and abilities
Level III Instructional design and development	All of the above plus
	Ability to design courseware, incorporating effective instructional principles
	Ability to develop (program) instructional software

applications in a specific field of knowledge. For educators, level II incorporates knowledge and skills in computer applications for instructional purposes in order to provide the practicing professional educator with the ability to use computers effectively within the discipline of education. Level II goes beyond the minimum requirements of computer literacy and focuses on discipline-specific knowledge. In education, the discipline-specific knowledge base includes principles of effective instruction, instructional design, and in a broader sense, educational psychology.

The third and highest level of interaction between computer knowledge and discipline knowledge is *instructional design and development.* This level includes skills, competencies, and knowledge in the design and development of instructional software, as well as the ability to develop and communicate theories, principles, and methods that link the fields of computer science and education.

This book is designed to facilitate the development of knowledge and skills at level II, the instructional applications literacy level, within the discipline of education. Since our purpose is to provide you with a set of basic principles, procedures, and methods for the use of computers to facilitate instruction in the schools, we will focus particularly on computer applications in instruction.

We believe that for the remainder of this century, the use of computers in schools will occur in human-oriented, teacher-directed learning environments. Within the context of the total school curriculum, informed educators should be able to make decisions about when computers should be used, for what purpose, and with what software applications. Strengths and weaknesses of a proposed instructional application should be considered within the context of what we know about instructional models that work, documented instructional procedures, and the time-tested principles of instructional design.

We assume that most teachers and students reading this text will have had some initial exposure to computers, through their own personal or educational experiences. Basic information about computers, such as the type or make of computer, computer capacities, ease of use, and cost, are topics that are coincidental to the main theme of the text. We will present some information about specific instructional applications to provide concrete examples of principles and procedures. Many of today's instructional software applications, however, will not be around tomorrow. They will be replaced by better, more appropriate applications, just as older textbooks are replaced by new and/or revised textbooks. We focus, therefore, not on specific programs but on the application of the underlying concepts and principles.

CURRENT INSTRUCTIONAL USES
OF COMPUTERS

In 1985, the Center for Social Organization of Schools, located at Johns Hopkins University, conducted an extensive survey of teachers and principals on the topic of instructional uses of computers. Approximately 8,000 teachers and principals were surveyed, providing a statistical representation of schools using computers in the United States. The educators surveyed reported that the use of computers has had a significant impact on instruction in four main areas: (1) increased student motivation, (2) increased student cooperation and independence, (3) increased learning opportunities for high-ability students, and (4) increased opportunities for low-ability students to master basic skills. Significantly, educators did not report the use of computers as contributing greatly to individualized and/or systematic instruction. Only a few reported the use of instructional management systems to conduct diagnostic instructional guidance and objective mastery instruction. At least in part, the lack of a reported impact on individualization and diagnostic instruction procedures reflects the lack of a conceptual framework for the use of computers as a tool for instruction. Certainly the availability of computers in the quantity needed to implement comprehensive instructional programs has also contributed to this finding.

When the educators included in the survey were asked to elaborate about other aspects of learning or instruction affected by the increased use of computers, six benefits were most often reported: (1) Computers help the development of logic, reasoning, and problem-solving competence; (2) computers help students who have particular learning handicaps, such as learning disabled students, Chapter I low-income students, and limited-English-speaking students; (3) computers help below-average students needing remediation; (4) computers help students in gifted and talented programs and other advanced students; (5) computers have value for instruction in mathematics; and (6) computers help improve self-confidence, provide a sense of accomplishment, and overcome computer anxiety. Although many experts have suggested that the availability of computers would dramatically change the organization and style of instruction in the typical classroom, the survey suggests that this is not happening at present. The majority of teachers indicated that classroom organization and routines have not changed as a result of using computers. The only notable change in the classroom teaching process attributed to the introduction of computers appears to be an increased amount of collaboration among students.

Although educators do not report a significant growth in the use of computers for instructional management and individualization of instruction, there does appear to be a significant use of computers for curriculum management and for evaluation. In a study supported by the Unisys Corporation and conducted by the University of North Carolina at Chapel Hill (1987), with a 60% response rate from 300 schools nationwide, 79% reported that they use computers to enter, store, retrieve, and print lists of mastery objectives for their school systems. Educators also reported a high level of computer use for the management of assessment and testing information. Sixty-seven percent of the systems responding reported that they use computers to store and retrieve test-results data and to print test-results reports.

When we review the results of the Johns Hopkins survey and the North Carolina survey together, we can make an important observation: Although schools use computers extensively to manage information about instruction (e.g., instructional objectives, minimal competencies, and achievement test results), they do not use the generated information on instructional progress to support and improve the instructional process in classrooms. The clear implication is that educators do not yet conceptually integrate computers into the actual process of instruction at the individual teacher and student level. Many educators using computers today have not moved beyond level I, or basic computer literacy, to level II, instructional applications literacy.

ASSUMPTIONS UNDERLYING INSTRUCTIONAL USES OF COMPUTERS

Even though the use of computers in schools is increasing rapidly, the development of an understanding of the relationship between computers and the school curriculum is not keeping pace. Many educators appear to need a better understanding of the use of computers in relationship to the instructional process. Certainly, some educational goals can be supported more appropriately with computers than can other educational goals. Likewise, some types of instructional content can be presented more effectively with computers than others. The assumptions on which this book is based, and which provide a frame of reference for understanding the content presented in this text are shown in Box 1.1.

Computers and Teachers

A basic assumption of this text is that the use of computers for instruction will facilitate the instructor's primary role—that of imparting knowledge. Computers will not dramatically change the organization of schools and

---

Box 1.1   The Use of Computers for Instruction: Underlying Assumptions

1. Computers will not replace teachers and/or instructors.
2. Computers can be used effectively to promote learning objectives associated with the acquisition of knowledge and comprehension.
3. A computer is a tool in the hands of the teacher or instructor, to assist with instruction and instructional management.
4. The characteristics of effective instruction are also the characteristics of effective computer-based instruction (CBI).
5. For the remainder of the twentieth century, one of the primary roles of computers in instruction will be enrichment, remediation, and the management of instructional information.

---

classrooms, at least not in the foreseeable future. Teachers will continue to be in charge of instruction and will continue to be the primary instructional decision maker. Instruction will continue to be human oriented, as opposed to machine oriented. In effect, the computer is an extension of the teacher's instructional and instructional-management capabilities. The teacher will decide when and how to use computers in instruction—with which pupils, for what purposes, and with what expectations. It has been demonstrated that computers can be used effectively for (1) direct instruction; (2) the management of information about instruction; and (3) assessment, diagnosis, and instructional planning.

Instructional Objectives

To better understand the processes of teaching and learning, some theorists have promoted specialized learning typologies which differentiate types of learning according to what is being learned (Good & Brophy, 1986). Most useful of these are the classifications established by Bloom (1971) and Gagne, Briggs and Wager (1988). Bloom's taxonomy includes the categories of knowledge, comprehension, application, analysis, synthesis, and evaluation. Gagne and Briggs's complementary categories are attitudes, motor skills, verbal information, intellectual skills, and cognitive strategies.

The evidence supporting the use of computers for instruction primarily emanates from studies and applications dealing with Bloom's categories of knowledge and comprehension and Gagne and Briggs's learning category of verbal information skills. We do not mean to suggest that computers cannot or should not be used to promote learning related to the other, higher-level categories. To date, however, many instructional applications, and subsequent evaluations of effectiveness, have avoided instruction aimed at the higher-order learning objectives. This may mean that computer-assisted instruction is reflecting only what educators spend most of their time teaching. As Good and Brophy (1984) point out, critical analysis of public school curricula typically reveals that a very high percentage of textbook content, practice exercises, and classroom activities in elementary and secondary schools focus on knowledge and comprehension levels. Little attention has been given to the higher levels of learning such as analysis, synthesis, and evaluation.

The Computer as an Instructional Tool

Webster defines *tool* as "something (an instrument or apparatus) used in performing an operation or necessary in the practice of a vocation or profession." Many textbooks and/or workshops on the use of computers in education focus on conveying information about computers—how they work, their various functions and capacities, and the different types of computers and computer software available. This book assumes that the reader has already reached level I computer literacy.

Just as a textbook is a tool for instruction, so is the computer. The computer is a medium that can be used to enhance the teacher's ability to deliver instruction. That is, in the hands of a teacher, this instructional medium becomes a tool for the implementation of instruction. Accordingly, we will talk in this text about teaching *with* the computer, and we will not directly address those topics that teach *about* the computer.

Effective Instruction and Computer-Based Instruction

Through the years, educational researchers have developed an extensive foundation of knowledge that establishes the parameters of effective schools and effective instruction. Most discussions on the use of computers in education, however, make no attempt to define the relationship between effective teaching and how computers might be used in instruction. What is known about effective instruction can clearly be used to guide and structure methods for using computers in the classroom. For example, the rich and extensive literature on mastery learning developed by Benjamin Bloom (1971, 1974, 1976) and others can potentially be used to develop a conceptual framework for the integration of computer-based instructional management programs. Computer-based instruction (CBI) software programs should be designed so that they are consistent with the basic principles of effective learning. In selecting appropriate software as well as in determining how to best use it for instruction, you should be guided by the principles of effective instruction.

Curriculum and Computers

The expected or desired instructional outcomes determine, at least in part, which types of curriculum activities are chosen for computer use. We must distinguish between CBI that supplements learning activities and CBI that substitutes for other modes of instruction. Supplemental CBI is usually presented by short (i.e., one-half hour) programs used to support or illustrate concepts (Chambers & Sprecher, 1983). Computer-based instruction that provides the primary instruction is used as a substitute for teacher-directed instruction. This form of CBI involves longer periods of time for pupil-computer interaction and usually includes graphics and data management. Computer-based instruction is not used as a substitute for regular instruction nearly as much as for a supplement to instruction.

In the survey by Becker (1987) mentioned earlier, designed to find out how elementary and secondary schools are actually using computers in the curriculum, significant differences were found between grade levels. As shown in Figure 1.1, from kindergarten through the eighth grade, computers are primarily used for enrichment instruction and

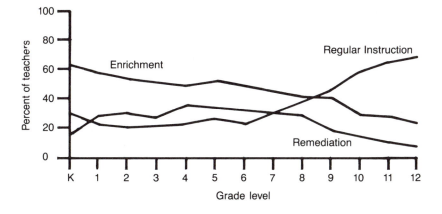

Figure 1.1. Function of computer activity for teachers—enrichment remediation, or regular instruction by grade level. (SOURCE: "Using computers for instruction," by J. H. Becker, *Byte,* February 1987. Reprinted by permission of the publisher.)

activities. There is also a significant remediation role from the first grade through the seventh grades. At the secondary level, by far the heaviest curriculum use is teaching *about* the computer, which includes computer literacy, computer science, and programming. Becker includes these topics under "regular instruction," but they are more appropriately labeled *computer instruction* so as to distinguish them from the use of computers to deliver primary instruction in academic subjects.

In keeping with the theme of this text, we will emphasize the use of the computer as an instructional tool. The curriculum areas of enrichment and remediation will be a primary focus. In addition, our curriculum applications will include supplemental direct instruction in academic content areas, so that the computer-based instructional activity we discuss can be used not only as enrichment or remediation but also as part of regular instruction.

The evidence available on the effects of CBI supports a focus on knowledge and comprehension outcomes. Kulik, Bangert, and Williams (1984) conducted one of the best known meta-analysis of studies on CBI effectiveness. They analyzed fifty-one studies of the effects of CBI on performance in final examinations and retention examinations. Both these variables traditionally emphasize knowledge and comprehension. Although procedures employed in the meta-analysis have been questioned (Clark, 1986), Kulik's findings have generally been accepted in support of CBI. The analysis showed that CBI raised final examination scores by approximately .32 standard deviations (a rise from the fiftieth to the sixty-third percentile). Very few studies examined by Kulik had results that favored conventional instruction.

These results suggest that in many instructional situations aimed at increasing knowledge and comprehension, CBI is better than, or just as good as, conventional instruction. Such a conclusion offers an array of potential instructional alternatives for educators. Teachers can become much more selective and flexible in the instructional activities that they engage in on a daily basis. We note with interest Kulik's suggestion that the effects of CBI seem especially clear in studies promoting the development of basic academic skills with pupils who have traditionally been classified as "disadvantaged." The CBI curriculum role of remediation, as reported by Becker, is clearly supported by Kulik's findings.

THE INSTRUCTIONAL MODEL, COMPUTERS, AND THE ORGANIZATION OF THIS BOOK

To begin the process of integrating what is known about effective instruction with the instructional use of computers, an instructional framework must be established. One of the most widely used instructional models was presented in the early 1960s by Glaser (1962). Glaser's basic model divides the instructional process into four main stages or components. Table 1.2 illustrates the relationship of Glaser's instructional model to the content in most of the chapters in this book.

Glaser's basic instructional model divides the instructional process into four main parts: (1) establishing instructional objectives, (2) determining entering behavior, (3) implementing instructional procedures, and (4) evaluating performance. As suggested by DeCecco (1968) the basic instructional model provides a straightforward and clear conceptualization of the instructional process. The use of a model also provides an organizing framework for various levels of information, such as facts, principles, and procedures related to the various components of the model.

The first instructional stage includes the establishment of the curricular scope and sequence, that is, the subjects, skill areas, and instructional objectives that define the curriculum. Once the curricular scope and sequence are established, the next step is to determine each student's abilities relative to the curriculum—a process referred to as *assessing entering behaviors.* Glaser's component of instructional procedures includes instructional planning and the establishment of individual objectives, followed by the actual instruction. Finally, evaluation of performance is undertaken to determine the extent to which the instructional objectives have been achieved.

The instructional model organizes the concepts, principles, and procedures that are involved in the use of computers for instruction. As shown in Table 1.2, chapter 2 provides a foundation for the remainder of the book by presenting the principles derived from what we know about

TABLE 1.2. INSTRUCTIONAL FRAMEWORK FOR COMPUTERS AND EFFECTIVE INSTRUCTION

Glaser's Instructional Model	Instructional Principles	Instructional Applications
Establishing instructional objectives	Chapter 2	Chapter 3 Chapter 4
Assessing entering behaviors	Chapter 3	Chapter 5
Instructional procedures	Chapter 2	Chapter 3
Performance assessment	Chapter 2	Chapter 4 Chapter 7

effective instruction in the context of the instructional uses of computers. The foundation for using computers will incorporate Glaser's classic stages or steps of instruction: (1) developing instructional plans and establishing instructional objectives; (2) assessing entry behaviors and tracking student progress; (3) implementing instructional procedures; and (4) assessing performance.

Supported by principles of instructional design, chapter 3, "Effective Courseware Design," discusses concepts important for the effective use of computers by the teacher. The chapter provides guidelines for the selection of software programs and their integration into the curriculum.

Chapter 4, "Instructional Management," addresses the first stage of Glaser's instructional model—establishing instructional objectives and developing instructional plans. This chapter discusses curricular scope and sequence, instructional objectives, and other concepts embedded in the mastery learning approach to instruction. Computer-based procedures available to manage instructional objectives and objective mastery information at the classroom level are also presented.

Perhaps one of the greatest uses of computers in education today is in assessment and evaluation. Computers are used to facilitate test administration, test scoring, and test analysis. These activities are represented in Glaser's second stage, assessing entry behaviors. Methods and procedures for these assessment activities in the use of computers are presented in chapter 5, "Assessment and Evaluation."

Chapter 6, "Special Learners and Special Applications," discusses computer applications in the instructional process for special education students. Topics included in this chapter are speech synthesizers for sight-impaired and multihandicapped students, as well as special software applications for gifted students.

Chapter 7, "Courseware Evaluation," presents methods and procedures to evaluate the contributions of instructional software.

The final chapter, chapter 8, "Computers and Instruction in the Schools of Tomorrow," discusses what to expect in the coming years, with the computer as a tool for effective and creative instruction.

It is no small task to attempt to organize and structure the current computer applications for instruction. The general topic of computer-based instruction is referred to by a number of different names. These include computer-assisted instruction (CAI), computer-assisted learning (CAL), computer-based education (CBE), and computer-based instruction (CBI). Although some computer science professionals may interpret the meaning of each of these labels differently, most educators use these terms interchangeably. This text emphasizes the use of computers for instruction and therefore uses the acronym *CBI*, which is used throughout the text to refer to the use of computers for direct instructional activities, that is, when the pupil is directly interacting with a computer for a learning-related goal.

Computer-managed instruction (CMI) refers to the general process of storing, retrieving, analyzing, and reporting instructionally related information. Sometimes *instructional management systems* is also used to refer to CMI. Computer-managed instruction should not be confused with computer-based management (CBM). Many educational agencies use CBM to manage administrative information such as budgets, inventories, personnel information, and student information. Computer-managed instruction relates directly to the instructional process because the information being managed has a direct bearing on the effectiveness and quality of instruction. These systems keep track of pupil performance levels, instructional objectives mastered, instructional objectives currently active, and suggested instructional activities.

PUTTING THE BOOK TO WORK

Read each of the following questions and briefly review the source pages indicated. Respond to the first question, in your mind or on paper, and then answer each succeeding question in the same manner. This dynamic process of putting the book to work for you will provide a summary of the content presented in the chapter.

Question	*Source*
1. Why are computers getting so much attention from educators today?	5–6
2. What are the major assumptions for using computers for instruction that underlie this book?	6–10
3. How does Glaser's instructional model relate to the contents of this book?	10–12
4. How do user competencies at level I differ from those at level II?	2–4
5. How does computer-managed instruction (CMI) support effective teaching, mastery learning, and individualized instruction?	12

CHAPTER 2

Principles of Effective Instruction and Computers in the Schools

Objectives

After reading this chapter, you should be able to do the following:

1. Explain the difference between instructional principles that are based on (a) consensus, (b) personal wisdom, and (c) and research.
2. Evaluate CBI programs by using criteria derived from research-based instructional principles.
3. Describe the implications of research-based instructional principles for developing, selecting, and using CBI programs.
4. Critique the criteria frequently used to evaluate CBI programs on the basis of research-based instructional principles.

INSTRUCTIONAL PRINCIPLES AND COMPUTER-BASED INSTRUCTION

We believe that all teaching and learning environments are human environments and that it does not make sense to talk about computer environments. We find it useful, however, to discuss the implications of using computers as tools in a human environment. Knowledge about effective instruction has obvious implications for designing and developing, selecting, and using CBI programs. An examination of the various criteria used to evaluate CBI programs suggests that this body of knowledge has, for the most part, been ignored. Computer-based instructional programs have rarely been evaluated in the context of effective teaching principles. Yet these principles are just as relevant to computer instruction as they are to teacher-presented instruction. In this chapter we will review for you the principles of effective teaching that have emerged from years of research in the area and point out how CBI software programs can be evaluated to ensure that the programs you select will embody these principles. This discussion will provide a set of effective evaluative standards for the selection of CBI software. Clark (1986) has rightfully observed that learning gains come from good instructional design and practice, not from the medium used to deliver instruction.

Computer-based instructional software should be consistent with the basic principles of learning, especially those principles supported by empirical research. Further, the instructional settings for the use of software programs should be consistent with these same principles.

When the characteristics of existing software programs are reviewed in terms of research-based instructional principles, the results are less favorable than anticipated. Many schools have shelves filled with seldom-used CBI programs, even though these programs were favorably reviewed under traditional criteria. Other programs are used in ways that are inconsistent with many of the basic principles of learning. Instructional principles need to be considered both in the design and development of CBI programs and in their use.

Regrettably, ineffective and inefficient CBI software programs and environments are easier to find than effective ones. The problem lies in the criteria that are generally used to assess software programs. Many of the criteria commonly found in textbooks and evaluation literature have little to do with student achievement. Even though many CBI programs have internal validity for their stated purposes, few of them provide directions or guidelines for their efficient use by teachers and others. In some situations, the conditions in the learning environment (e.g., a teacher who is not organized or students who are misbehaving) preclude students from taking advantage of effective programs.

The principles presented in this chapter are based on a review of more than 650 studies of effective instruction (Group for the Study of Effective Teaching, 1983). Most of the supporting research has been conducted during the past decade. Nearly all the studies supporting these principles were conducted in regular classrooms under normal conditions and collected data by direct observation. Most of the studies were attempts to answer the critical question, "What is it that effective teachers do that less effective teachers do not do or do not do as well?" A common procedure has been to identify teachers who have been exceptionally effective for several consecutive years and to compare their teaching behaviors with those of less effective teachers. The results from a very large number of studies conducted by different investigators in different states and different countries are remarkably similar.

Although the studies have not been evenly distributed across different age groups and different subject areas, there are some generic instructional findings that appear to apply in a large variety of contexts. Although these findings usually apply both to the design and development of CBI programs and to their use, most of these principles apply more to one of these than to the other.

The sixteen generic instructional principles that we believe are critical to the design, development, selection, and use of effective computer software programs for the classroom are listed in Box 2.1. In the next section, each principle will be introduced followed by a statement of the principle; a brief review of the most pertinent research; and finally, most importantly, a discussion of the implications of that

---

Box 2.1   Research-Based Instructional Principles Related to the Design and Development of CBI Software

1. Beginning lessons with review
2. Beginning lessons with an introduction
3. Presenting instruction fluently and precisely
4. Using understandable language and concepts
5. Using relevant examples and demonstrations
6. Ensuring high rates of success
7. Presenting instruction at a brisk pace
8. Making smooth transitions within and between lessons
9. Making assignments and instructions clear
10. Summarizing the main points of the lesson
11. Maintaining reasonable standards
12. Checking student performance routinely
13. Posing questions one at a time
14. Providing instructional feedback
15. Affirming correct responses
16. Providing sustained feedback after incorrect responses

principle for software design, selection, and use. You will find criteria for software evaluation at the end of the chapter. These criteria are derived from the principles of effective instruction discussed in this chapter.

RESEARCH-BASED INSTRUCTIONAL PRINCIPLES RELATED TO COMPUTER-BASED INSTRUCTION

Beginning Lessons with Review

Students learn more when lessons and activities begin with a review of previous material. Lessons and instructional activities should begin with the recall of main points of previous lessons or earlier experiences that are related to the content to be taught. This review requires more than just reminding students of what they have studied or telling them how important it is to remember earlier lessons.

In a series of studies (Emmer et al., 1982; Fortune, 1967; Kozma, 1982; Stanford Center for Research & Development, 1975), researchers found that students achieve more in instructional settings in which lessons were begun with an initial review of previous material. Exercises and questions should prompt the recall of previously learned information and skills that are relevant to the present task. Students get on task more quickly and remain on task for a longer period of time in those classrooms in which teachers begin with a review. Also teachers who present more structured lessons tend to begin with an initial review more often than do teachers who use a less structured format. These findings have been supported by studies done at all levels from elementary school through college.

Beginning a lesson with a review helps the learner recall and review information and skills that are pertinent to the present learning. There is probably a direct relationship between the need for review and the elapsed time between the study of related material and the present learning. The longer it has been since the learner studied relevant information and skills, the greater the need for stimulated recall. Many of us know from our own experiences that after having been away from school for a few months we must conduct a review of previously learned material for new learning to be efficient. Most learners find this true even when the elapsed time is much briefer. Conversely, when the elapsed time between the previous study and the present learning is short, the amount of necessary review is generally less.

Effective CBI programs begin lessons with a review of relevant information and skills. *These programs generally use highly structured formats into which it is relatively easy to incorporate a review com-*

ponent. If students are learning to write simple programs in BASIC, for example, the instructional program might appropriately review the concepts of GOTO and FOR . . . NEXT, on the assumption that these had been studied earlier. The screen for such a review might resemble that in Figure 2.1. **Look for an initial review feature when you select software.**

Research evidence suggests that learning is more efficient when the program stimulates recall of relevant information and skills before presenting new content. If you select an instructional program that does not include an initial review, you will need to provide it yourself before your students access the program. When students are working at different levels, this can be a difficult and time-consuming task for you.

Beginning Lessons with an Introduction

Students learn more when lessons and activities are introduced and learning objectives are specified, when appropriate. Tasks should be clearly and concisely explained at the beginning of a lesson. Lesson

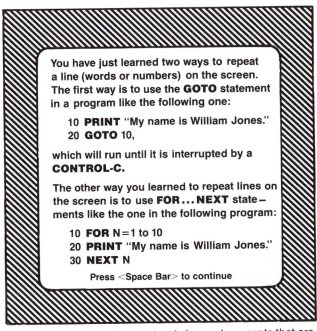

Figure 2.1. A screen showing previously learned concepts that are presented for review purposes.

introductions can also include the purpose or goal of the lesson, an overview of the content, and/or a specific order or pattern that the lesson will follow.

Studies that evaluate the effect of properly introducing the lesson include Anderson et al., 1979; Emmer, Evertson, & Anderson, 1980; Emmer et al., 1981; Fisher et al., 1978; Kozma, 1982; and Stanford Center for Research and Development, 1975. Just as providing an introductory description of the lesson or its activities has been correlated positively with high achievement, failure to provide such an introduction has been negatively related to achievement. The extent to which teachers explain the nature and objectives of the lessons they are about to teach has also been correlated directly to the amount of time students spend on task. Research indicates that students do better when teachers describe what they are expected to learn from the content presented. Content can be introduced in a number of ways, but some form of introduction should be made with every lesson. Again, research suggests that this practice of introduction is more often used in highly structured lessons than in less structured ones.

Effective CBI programs describe the lesson objectives and explain the purpose of the lesson. *The learner might be told, for example, that he or she will learn how to write a simple program that will compare two or more letters, numbers, words, or statements. The lesson introduction might also describe the exact sequence in which lesson segments will be covered. The screen might resemble that in Figure 2.2.* **Look for an introductory segment in the instructional software you select.**

If you select an instructional program that does not include an introduction, you will need to explain the objectives and patterns of the content to the students yourself.

Presenting Instruction Fluently and Precisely

Students learn more when verbal content is precise and is presented fluently. Common sense suggests, and research confirms, that students learn more when difficult words and long phrases are avoided, transitions are made smoothly, and a lesson moves forward with minimal interruptions and distractions. Presenting information smoothly and precisely has been consistently related to student achievement (Hiller, Fisher, and Kaess, 1969; Land and Smith, 1979; Smith, 1977; Smith and Cotten, 1980; Smith and Edmonds, 1978). Several studies have demonstrated that teacher vagueness and lack of fluency consistently correlate with lower levels of student achievement. The most effective instruction minimizes the use of ambiguous terms and uses approximations only when they are appropriate to the lesson content. Effective instruction minimizes the use of assuming statements ("as you all know" or "it is obvious that") and

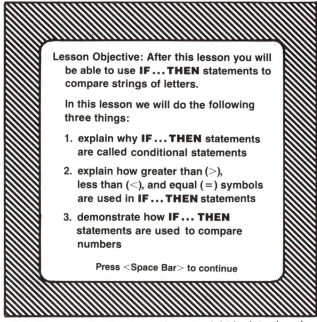

Lesson Objective: After this lesson you will be able to use **IF...THEN** statements to compare strings of letters.

In this lesson we will do the following three things:

1. explain why **IF...THEN** statements are called conditional statements

2. explain how greater than (>), less than (<), and equal (=) symbols are used in **IF...THEN** statements

3. demonstrate how **IF...THEN** statements are used to compare numbers

Press <Space Bar> to continue

Figure 2.2. A screen showing how a lesson might be introduced.

indeterminate statements ("pretty soon" or "before very long"). Effective instruction also keeps repetition of words or phrases to a minimum.

Research shows that the importance of presenting instruction fluently and precisely is consistent across subject areas and grade levels.

Effective CBI programs should provide instruction as clearly and precisely as possible. *Computer programs have an innate strength, in that they are always and invariably consistent. Once language is entered, it never changes. Their weakness, however, is that students cannot seek clarification from the program itself, in most cases, but must ask the teacher for help if they don't understand a word or phrase. Such attempts to seek clarification can be disruptive. Those developing CBI programs should seek critiques from subject matter specialists and also from "naive" users who are members of the intended audience to make sure vocabulary and language are appropriate.*

Carefully designed software can avoid problems of vagueness, lack of fluency, and lack of "forward motion" that hinder student achievement. **You should look for software that uses clear and precise language, that moves logically from one segment to the next, and that avoids unnecessary interruptions or distractions,** including graphic displays.

Using Understandable Language and Concepts

Students learn more when lessons and instructional activities are presented through concepts and language that are understandable and appropriate to the intended audience. Studies have consistently shown that language should be not only clear and precise but also understandable and appropriate; such instructional appropriateness is related to student on-task behavior, social behavior, and achievement (Cooley & Leinhardt, 1978; Emmer, Evertson, & Anderson, 1980; Emmer et al., 1981; Gage et al., 1968; Leinhardt, 1977). The critical issue is the level at which lessons are presented; content vocabulary and expressions must be familiar to students or must allow students to relate the lesson content to their own experience. The intended audience for instruction consists not of experts in a given field but of students for whom the lesson content may be entirely new. One method of making instructional material understandable to students is asking questions at appropriate intervals, asking them clearly, and asking only one question at a time rather than compounding questions, which students often find confusing.

Effective CBI programs present content at a level appropriate for the intended audience. *Authors of CBI programs should field-test their programs with members of the intended audience to ensure that the content presented is at an appropriate level of difficulty. Programs are sometimes written with several levels of difficulty, so that students may select the path they will follow in keeping with their own needs. You might want to look for this feature if your students vary greatly in ability or academic background. In general, however,* **look for programs that present content at a level consistent with the ability of your students.**

To evaluate whether or not a program uses vocabulary and concepts appropriate for your students, you will need to observe student responses that imply understanding, using standard measures such as oral questions, quizzes, homework papers, and the like.

A particular strength of CBI programs is that they generally require a student response to each question before they move on to the next, and that they require that response from every student—not simply from the one with a raised hand.

Using Relevant Examples and Demonstrations

Students learn more when relevant examples and demonstrations are provided to illustrate concepts and skills. Studies done with students ranging from kindergarten to college indicate a consistent and relatively strong relationship between the number of relevant examples and demonstrations used and student achievement (Armento, 1976; Emmer et al.,

1981; Evans & Guyman, 1978; Gage et al., 1968; Smith, 1977). Studies also indicate that a higher number of irrelevant examples is associated with a lower level of student achievement.

Research suggests that effective teachers use more examples for difficult concepts and principles than they do for less difficult ones. Examples can be either planned or spontaneously generated during the course of the lesson; evidence shows that one is no more or less effective than the other.

Effective CBI lessons use examples and demonstrations; the better the examples, the better the lesson. *You should require a particularly good use of examples in CBI programs since software developers have ample opportunity to devise and include appropriate ones. Software developers are not "thinking on their feet," as teachers must often do. Further, developers have the opportunity to test their chosen examples and replace them if necessary.* **Look for CBI lessons that include effective examples and demonstrations, particularly when lesson content is difficult.**

Ensuring High Rates of Success

Students learn more when they are able to handle tasks and questions with high rates of success. Researchers have found that high-success activities are often associated with higher levels of student on-task behavior and more appropriate student social behavior (Emmer et al., 1981; Emmer et al., 1982; Fisher et al., 1980; Fisher et al., 1978; Kozma, 1982). Students in the most successful classes rarely if ever experience less than moderate success rates. In the most successful classes, all students experience high success rates.

A teacher's ability to design high-success lessons depends on his or her knowledge of the subject matter as well as knowledge of the students' rate of learning. Many teachers who have an excellent understanding of subject matter are unable to plan high-success activities because they don't clearly understand their students' rate of learning; not uncommonly, classrooms contain many students who are highly involved in the learning process, and who achieve moderate to high rates of success, and other students who appear to be lost or uninvolved.

Effective CBI lessons are designed to ensure moderate to high success rates. *This is an obvious strength of computer instruction since programs can be developed that will not allow students to proceed at a rate beyond their own abilities. Good programs are ones that have been field-tested with the intended audience, and which provide appropriate feedback for successful students and allow unsuccessful students options to obtain success at a slower pace.* **Look for programs that are designed to ensure success for students who learn at different rates.**

Presenting Instruction at a Brisk Pace

Students learn more when lessons are presented at a brisk pace and when teachers slow instruction if necessary for student understanding but avoid unnecessary slowdowns. Research conducted at all grade levels consistently has shown that students learn more when instruction proceeds at a relatively fast pace (Becker, 1977; Becker & Gersten, 1983; Cooley & Leinhardt, 1978; Gersten, Carmine & Williams, 1982; Good & Grouws, 1979; McDonald, 1976). At least one study indicates that students in social studies classrooms learn more when instruction proceeds at a moderate rate, and several other studies suggest that a fast pace of instruction correlates with high student achievement. Contrary to the popular belief that slow students will suffer when the pace of instruction is increased, studies suggest that *all* students learn more from fast-paced instruction, provided that the instruction is at the appropriate level.

Most researchers agree that the pace of instruction in the typical classroom is too slow. Students in faster-paced classrooms spend more time on task, participate more, and give more correct responses.

Interruptions, of course, slow down the pace of instruction; teachers cannot maintain a rapid instructional pace if the intercom comes on frequently, if unexpected visitors arrive, if the teacher must frequently add explanations or directions to material that has already been presented, or if students misbehave.

Effective CBI programs move quickly and avoid unnecessary interruptions. *CBI programs have several advantages over teachers when it comes to instructional pace. First, they are generally used by students individually, so that each student can regulate the pace to meet his or her needs. Second, CBI programs can be designed to eliminate unnecessary pauses, repetitions, or interruptions. If the principal arrives to talk to the teacher, students may nevertheless proceed with the lesson. Finally, CBI programs do not permit single students or small groups to dominate the learning process.* **Look for CBI programs that provide self-paced instruction and that minimize pauses and interruptions.**

Be careful to avoid those programs that violate the principle of pace by using time-consuming techniques (songs, graphics, elaborate feedback) to provide informational responses to students about their performances. When students answer questions, the computer response should be quick and clear. Research suggests that, over the long run, students learn more if they receive prompt feedback and move on to the next task, rather than being forced to wait for long and elaborate responses. The strength of CBI is in its ability to provide self-paced learning; unnecessary graphics or audio feedback denies that strength.

Making Smooth Transitions within and Between Lessons

Students learn more when transitions between lessons and instructional activities within lessons are made efficiently and smoothly. A number of empirical studies have concluded that students learn more when activity shifts require a minimum of time (Anderson, Evertson, & Brophy, 1979; Arlin, 1979; Emmer et al., 1981; Emmer et al., 1982; Kounin et al., 1966; Smith & Cotten, 1980). Transitions are often classified into major and minor. Major transitions are those that occur when instruction moves from one lesson to another or one activity to another (group discussion to viewing a film, for instance); minor transitions are those made within lessons (shift from a discussion of Eskimo economy to Eskimo religion). Research conducted at several grade levels shows that transitions are smoother and more efficient when they have been planned in advance. Classes in which transitions occur most smoothly are those in which teachers provide cues or signals that transitions are about to occur and in which transition routines have been established.

Intervention studies reveal that teachers can be taught how to make smooth and efficient transitions, and they can reduce student misbehavior when they learn these techniques. Frequent interruptions and slowdowns occur in classrooms where instruction is fragmented and unconnected.

Effective CBI programs make clear and smooth transitions from one part of a lesson to another. *You will no doubt need to help students actually change from one instructional program to another, but transitions within programmed material can be designed to move smoothly and efficiently. Authors have ample opportunity to program in the kinds of cues and signals that help students move from one part of a lesson or one activity to another. Good CBI programs avoid premature transitions; they make sure all appropriate material has been covered and **understood** before students are permitted to move on. Good CBI programs also avoid unnecessary returns to prior activities or information.* **Look for programs that provide cues for transitions between one activity or segment and another and that indicate clearly how the next material follows logically from that which precedes it.**

Making Assignments and Instructions Clear

Students learn more when clear and concise assignments and directions are provided. Studies at various grade levels have found a consistent relationship between clarity in giving directions and making assignments and student achievement (Emmer, Evertson, & Anderson, 1980; Emmer et al., 1981; Emmer et al., 1982). Effective teachers consistently are clear and concise in providing students with information about how to do the lesson and what is expected of them. Effective teachers space directions when two or more assignments are given, and they help students remember assignments by writing them out, especially in the case of complex assignments. Effective teachers also ask students questions to determine whether or not their instructions have been understood.

Effective CBI programs include clear directions and assignments. *Obviously, an inherent strength of computer instruction is that all assignments and directions are written out, and students can return to them (in most cases) at will by accessing prior screens.* **Look for programs that provide assignments one at a time and ask questions of the user to determine whether or not the assignments are understood.**

Summarizing the Main Points of the Lesson

Students learn more when the main points of the lesson are summarized at the end of the lesson or instructional activity. Research findings have consistently reported a relationship between reviewing and summarizing lesson content and student achievement (Armento, 1976; Emmer et al., 1982; Stanford Center for Research and Development, 1975; Wright & Nuthall, 1970). The more effectively teachers review and summarize, and the more time devoted to this activity, the higher the student achievement. Summarizations can be carried out in many different ways: Some teachers merely recap the main points of a lesson; some may require that students recall the most important information; others may do quick check quizzes. Whether the review is achieved through summarizing, restating, or rephrasing main ideas, its importance is undeniable.

Effective CBI lessons include a summary of key points at the end of the lesson. *Again, a strength of computer instruction is that the summary, once programmed, is always available. The computer program never runs out of time or forgets a key point because of an interruption in the classroom. Figure 2.3 provides an example of a lesson summarized by a number of questions which the user must answer in order to sign off the program.* **Look for lessons that include summaries, if not after each section of content, certainly at the end of the program.** *Particularly good are those programs that demand student input to make sure that key points have been understood.*

Maintaining Reasonable Standards

Students learn more when clear, firm, and reasonable standards are maintained. Determining due dates and standards of accomplishment is related positively not only to student academic achievement but also to

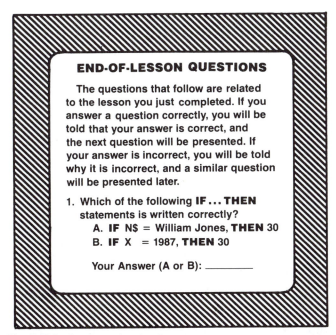

END-OF-LESSON QUESTIONS

The questions that follow are related to the lesson you just completed. If you answer a question correctly, you will be told that your answer is correct, and the next question will be presented. If your answer is incorrect, you will be told why it is incorrect, and a similar question will be presented later.

1. Which of the following **IF ... THEN** statements is written correctly?
   A. **IF** N$ = William Jones, **THEN** 30
   B. **IF** X = 1987, **THEN** 30

   Your Answer (A or B): _____

Figure 2.3. A screen showing how a lesson might be summarized by asking questions.

student on-task behavior; conversely, it is negatively related to disruptive student behavior in the classroom (Anderson et al., 1980; Borg & Ascione, 1982; Emmer, 1981; Emmer et al., 1982; Evertson, Anderson, & Brophy, 1978). Teachers who establish rules and procedures for appropriate student behavior are also often teachers who establish and enforce due dates and standards of academic performance. A study of mathematics classrooms indicates that teachers who did a better job of maintaining standards and due dates also showed more concern for student achievement and gave students more academic encouragement. Another study found that more effective teachers conveyed academic purposefulness by holding students accountable for their work, while reminding them frequently of their assignments and of the amount of time left to complete them.

Effective CBI programs adapt to student capabilities and hold students accountable for the work they do. *Obviously, computers cannot establish and enforce due dates for assignments. They can, however, provide segments that ensure that students actually do the work presented (through questions or review quizzes). Programs can ensure that*

students do not proceed if they have not yet mastered prior instruction.
Look for programs that help you enforce standards and due dates by requiring students to demonstrate their mastery of the material presented and, perhaps, by dividing the content of the lesson to fit your classroom schedule.

Checking Student Performance Routinely

Students learn more when teachers circulate during classroom assignments to check all student performances. Several studies indicate that effective teachers monitor student performance during independent work more often than less effective teachers (Emmer et al., 1981; Emmer et al., 1982; Fisher et al., 1978; McConnell, 1977). Teachers who did more academic monitoring had students who spent more time on task and were less disruptive. One effective way of monitoring, obviously, is to move about the room and observe the work of all students. A key word here is *all*, not simply those students who volunteer. Effective teachers remain alert to those students who need attention and distribute their time accordingly, but they recognize that all students must have work checked periodically.

Effective CBI programs routinely check for learner understanding. *A computer doesn't need to roam the room to check each student's work; only one student at a time responds to an instructional program on a single computer terminal. The task of monitoring work in a CBI program, then, requires the inclusion of segments that routinely check the user's progress in terms of understanding material presented. Checking a student's progress as he makes his or her way through the program, however, remains primarily your responsibility. Teachers need to check the work and progress of all students, and to do so on a regular basis.* **Look for programs that include periodic monitors—quizzes or questions—of student progress.**

Posing Questions One at a Time

Students learn more when questions are posed one at a time. Asking questions is an important monitoring skill, and effective teachers use questions regularly to assess student understanding. Research suggests that when teachers pose two or more questions before asking for a response, students are confused and achieve at a lower level. (Wright & Nuthall, 1970). Asking one question at a time correlates with positive achievement.

Effective CBI programs pose questions one at a time. *Good CBI programs can provide the opportunity for each student to give a correct* *answer before being presented with another question.* **Look for lessons that demand that students respond to each question asked before proceeding.**

Providing Instructional Feedback

Students learn more when instructional feedback on the correctness of their work is provided. Research suggests that teachers should provide students with prompt feedback on their in-class work (Gersten et al., 1982; Good & Grouws, 1979; Evertson et al., 1978; Hughes, 1973; Stallings, 1978). Such feedback is important whether it is in response to seatwork, group work, or answers to teachers' questions. Teachers should give specific and sincere instructional feedback. Ambiguous comments such as "okay" are used in a wide variety of ways in the classroom and are easily misinterpreted by students.

Studies have consistently shown a positive relationship between the provision of instructional feedback and student achievement. More effective teachers, research suggests, give more instructional feedback.

Effective CBI programs provide all students with prompt, sincere, and specific feedback on a regular basis. *Preplanned instruction like CBI can do this more effectively and more objectively than classroom teachers. Since the instruction in CBI is individualized, students can easily receive prompt feedback. Software designers can also avoid nondiscriminative and ambiguous comments that are characteristic of many classrooms.* **Look for lessons in which regular, prompt, and specific feedback is provided.**

Affirming Correct Responses

Students learn more when correct responses are affirmed appropriately and instruction moves on. Student responses to teacher questions can obviously take several forms: appropriate, inappropriate or incorrect, "I don't know," or silence. Several studies have examined the impact of how teachers respond to correct student responses (Anderson et al., 1979; Eggert, 1978; Evertson et al., 1978; Kounin, 1970; Wright & Nuthall, 1970). Research from a variety of grade levels generally indicates that students learn more when their correct responses are affirmed quickly and instruction moves forward. Some studies suggest that students learn more when no response is given to correct answers than when more elaborate responses are provided. (This finding does not appear to apply to young children from socioeconomically lower homes, however.) One study indicates that children learn more when teachers follow correct responses by asking a new question rather than elaborating on the correct answer.

Another study found that students achieve more when teachers explain to the whole class how a correct answer has been derived; for this to be effective, however, the teacher must avoid explaining too much or too often.

In general, simple affirmation of correct responses seems preferable in most cases. Teachers should avoid needless repetition or elaboration of student responses, should communicate to students that they are expected to provide correct answers, and should demonstrate that no fuss will be made over answers.

Effective CBI programs confirm correct responses and move on. *CBI programs lend themselves ideally to providing the kind of response that research indicates is desirable—simple affirmation. Good CBI programs avoid needless repetition and elaboration when it is unlikely to benefit learners. Elaboration may be appropriate for higher-achieving students; you are the best judge of your students' abilities. Instructional programs can be adapted to provide more elaboration on correct answers when this seems desirable.*

As we mentioned earlier, many existing CBI programs do not provide simple affirmations to correct student answers. Rather, they use graphics and gimmicks in an attempt to enhance student interest and motivation. Research indicates, however, that those gimmicks probably do not enhance achievement and in fact slow the pace of instruction, thereby hindering student interest. Students need to know if they have provided a correct response, but they do not need to be entertained each time they do so.

Providing Sustained Feedback
after Incorrect Responses

Students learn more when sustaining feedback is provided after an incorrect response or no response by probing, repeating the question, giving a clue, or allowing more time. Not all student responses are correct, of course. Research indicates that when students fail to respond or when they give incorrect answers, teachers should provide sustained interaction with those students (Crawford et al., 1976; Gage et al., 1968; Martin, Yeldman & Anderson, 1980; Rowe, 1974; Stallings, 1978; Webb, 1982). Teachers can do this in a variety of ways: supportively probing, providing cues, repeating the question, rephrasing the question, or allowing more time for the student to answer. Three different studies indicate that providing sustained feedback to students who fail to respond is consistently related to student achievement in different subject areas. Other studies indicate that students who answer incorrectly derive equal benefit from sustaining feedback.

Many teachers intentionally or unintentionally provide terminal feedback or negate a student's incorrect answer by immediately supplying the correct answer or calling on another student or by simply saying, "No, that's wrong." Evidence indicates that such negative feedback negatively affects student achievement. Students should receive a sufficient amount of time to respond to questions, and if they are unable to provide a correct response, the teacher should provide guides, probes, or more time. Teacher feedback should indicate the degree of "correctness" or appropriateness in the student's response, and teachers should avoid calling immediately on another student.

Effective CBI programs provide cues and probes when students answer questions incorrectly as well as reasonable periods of time in which students can respond. *These programs never call on another student when the first is having difficulty with an answer; computers can have infinite patience. Good programs can provide an indication of the degree to which a student's answer is correct or appropriate.* **Look for programs that are designed to help students arrive at a correct answer, rather than simply telling them they're wrong.**

SUMMARY

In the past two decades, numerous studies have examined the relationship between various teaching practices and student achievement. Researchers have identified certain practices that consistently relate to student achievement, regardless of age or subject matter. Most important among these are practices that are clearly under the control of the teacher. These practices have obvious implications for the selection, design, development, and use of computer-based instructional programs. Nonetheless, they have generally been ignored by those who develop CBI programs and by those who use these programs. For the most effective use of computers in instruction, these practices must serve as basic principles for both those who develop CBI programs and those who select and use them in the classroom.

The teaching practices discussed in this chapter are based on a review of more than 650 studies of classroom teaching. The chapter presents sixteen instructional principles that the authors believe are critical to learning. Each principle is described and discussed, and supporting research is cited; implications are suggested for the design and development, selection, and use of CBI programs. The following questions provide a quick guide for evaluating educational software. For more expanded guidelines, see the Longman Courseware Evaluation Checklist in chapter 7.

Questions for Evaluating the Educational Feasibility of Instructional Software

1. Does the program *begin with a review* of previously learned material?	Yes	No
2. Does the program *begin with an introduction* to the lesson?	Yes	No
3. Is the content of the program *presented fluently and precisely?*	Yes	No
4. Are the *concepts and language* in the program *appropriate* for the intended users?	Yes	No
5. Are *relevant examples and demonstrations* used in the program?	Yes	No
6. Does it appear that the intended users will experience *high rates of success* with the program?	Yes	No
7. Does it appear that the content is presented at an *appropriately brisk pace?*	Yes	No
8. Are the *transitions* in the program *efficient and smooth?*	Yes	No
9. Are *assignments* in the program *clear and concise?*	Yes	No
10. Are lessons concluded with a *wrap-up or summary?*	Yes	No
11. Does the program specify *clear and reasonable standards?*	Yes	No
12. Does the program *check student performance routinely?*	Yes	No
13. Are *questions posed one at a time?*	Yes	No
14. Do students receive *regular feedback* on the correctness of their work?	Yes	No
15. Are *correct responses confirmed quickly* and appropriately?	Yes	No
16. Do students receive *sustained feedback after incorrect answers?*	Yes	No

PUTTING THE BOOK TO WORK

Read each of the following questions and briefly review the source pages indicated. Respond to these questions, either in your mind or on paper. This process will provide a summary of the content presented in this chapter.

Question	*Source*
1. What is meant by "research-based instructional principles"?	16–17
2. Why is a classroom in which students are using computers for instruction still called a "human" learning environment?	15–16
3. What is the rationale for using instructional principles derived from research on classroom teaching to select and evaluate CBI programs?	16
4. What are the major shortcomings of the criteria commonly used to evaluate CBI programs?	16
5. What are five instructional principles that can be carried out more effectively by the computer than by the classroom teacher?	22–31
6. Why are so many CBI programs purchased by schools seldom used?	16
7. What are the characteristics of some CBI programs that result in the pace of instruction being too slow?	24
8. Why is it important to begin a lesson with a review?	18, 30
9. What is the difference between a major and a minor transition in computer-based instruction?	25
10. What are the characteristics of "effective feedback"?	29
11. What should be done in a CBI program when a student gives a correct answer to a question?	29–30
12. What should be done in a CBI program when a student is unable to respond correctly to a question in the program?	30–31

CHAPTER 3

Effective Courseware Design

Objectives

After completing this chapter, you should be able to do the following:

1. Describe three primary types of CBI.
2. Identify effective preinstructional displays.
3. Identify effective instructional displays.
4. Identify effective postinstructional displays.
5. Describe principles for screen layout.
6. Describe principles for the design of the instructional stimulus.
7. Describe principles for the design of directions to the student.
8. Describe principles for providing learning guidance.

INTRODUCTION: THE IMPORTANCE OF GOOD DESIGN

If students are to learn from computer-based instruction (CBI), the lessons delivered by computer must be carefully conceived and designed. Although many studies have demonstrated that CBI can be an effective form of instruction, these studies also indicate that simply placing some material on a computer will not improve its effectiveness (Clark, 1983). The computer itself does not improve the quality of instruction that is programmed into its memory.

The study of what makes CBI effective is remarkably similar to the study of what makes instruction effective. Computer-based instruction is simply one form of instruction, one way of storing and delivering instruction. Thus, CBI can deliver very poor instruction as easily as it can deliver very good instruction. The difference between poor instruction and good instruction has little to do with computers and much to do with how the instruction is designed. In chapter 2 we reviewed principles of effective instruction that can be applied to CBI. In this chapter we discuss how effective CBI lessons are designed, based on research studies and many years of experience.

The design and development of CBI lessons is a very time-consuming process. Typically it takes over a hundred hours to produce one hour of effective CBI. It is just as unreasonable to expect all teachers to produce their own CBI, as it is unreasonable to expect all teachers to produce their own textbooks and instructional films. More often, teachers will be selecting CBI lessons to fit their instructional needs, not producing them. However, the suggestions in this chapter are equally useful for both situations—those in which CBI lessons are being produced, and those in which they are being selected. The features that you should incorporate into the design of effective CBI are the same features you should look for when selecting CBI that someone else has designed. The principles of effective CBI remain the same.

CBI LESSON DEVELOPMENT

Effective CBI lessons are carefully developed, and most follow a systematic instructional design model, such as the one shown in Figure 3.1.

If you are developing CBI lessons, you should follow an approach similar to that described here. If you are selecting CBI materials for classroom use, you should be aware of the processes followed in development. Note that in developing CBI lessons, much work is done before any materials are actually entered on a computer. Quality, to a large extent, is due to the care taken in the developmental stage.

Several steps in the developmental process are crucial to effective CBI. The CBI lesson should be based on a needs assessment or task analysis, so that the outcomes sought in the lesson will have a basis in the lives of the students. Further, these instructional outcomes must be stated in clear, unambiguous terms, so that all users understand the expected outcomes in the same way. Lessons should employ clearly stated

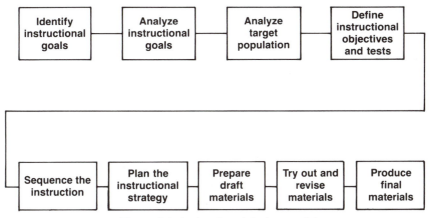

Figure 3.1. Instructional design model

objectives, so that the CBI developers, teachers, and students will all understand the purpose of the lesson.

The CBI lessons should be geared to the specific students who make up the group for whom the lesson is being developed or selected. Virtually every model describing how to design instruction includes a consideration of the students for whom the instruction is planned (Andrews & Goodson, 1980). Depending on the characteristics of the audience, the CBI lesson might cover different content or might present the content in a different fashion. This specificity of design is the same as you would find in other fields, for example, speech writing. Both the content and presentation of a speech about physics would differ if we were talking to a group of fourth-grade students, high school seniors, physics majors in college, professors of physics, or the general public. Just as a speech would differ according to the audience, so also would a CBI lesson on physics differ according to the audience. Effective instruction, like effective communications, demands that you plan for your particular audience.

The content to be included in the CBI lesson should be derived through a careful consideration of what is required of students in order to reach the objectives of the lesson. Once the lesson objectives are identified, they can be analyzed to determine the instructional content that will support their achievement. Through such procedures, the lesson's objectives are broken down into their component parts—the knowledge and skills necessary for their mastery—and CBI lessons should focus on these. By eliminating extraneous content, CBI can reduce learning time, a promising accomplishment of the use of CBI as an instructional medium. Most studies report that CBI instruction results in a considerable savings in the time required for students to master the stated objectives of the lesson (Kulik, Bangert, & Williams, 1983).

Designers of CBI should pay close attention to the means by which students are expected to learn. Specifically, the CBI lesson designer must ask, "How might I best communicate *this* content to *these* students?" To respond accurately, the designer must consider both what is known about how people learn and also what makes effective instruction. Chapter 2 of this text presents information about effective teaching practices and their implications for the design of CBI lessons. When planning CBI lessons, you should incorporate these practices into your designs. When reviewing CBI lessons for classroom use, you should make sure that the lessons you select include these effective teaching practices.

Once developed, CBI lessons should be formatively evaluated and revised. Each lesson should be tried out with its intended population of learners. Then by examining whether students master each objective, you can determine the effectiveness of the CBI lesson.

LESSON ORGANIZATION

Effective CBI lessons are tightly designed CBI lessons; rambling prose does not have a place in CBI. Rather the content in CBI lessons must be organized in a consistent manner, and this organization must be made known to the student (Hannum, 1988). Perhaps the best starting place for a discussion of lesson organization is to describe the basic types of CBI lessons—drill and practice, tutorial, and simulation.

Drill and Practice

In drill and practice CBI, the learner is first presented with a question, enters the answer, and receives confirmation about the correctness of the answer. Figure 3.2 shows the logic that underlies drill and practice CBI lessons.

Drill and practice CBI accounts for much of the available instructional software in most subject areas. Indications are that drill and practice CBI is effective in promoting learning for most learners in most subject areas. In a drill and practice CBI lesson the learners are practicing the use of knowledge or skills that have been previously acquired. Drill and practice CBI is less useful for initial instruction.

Tutorial

In tutorial CBI lessons the learner is given information to assist with the acquisition of new knowledge and skills. Tutorial programs carry on a continual dialog with the learner. A tutorial program first presents new

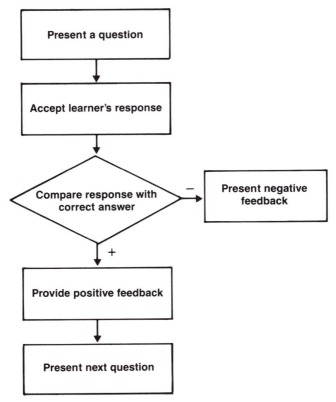

Figure 3.2. Basic drill and practice model

information to the learner and then provides the opportunity for practice in using the new information. The logic underlying a tutorial program is shown in Figure 3.3.

The tutorial program presents information, asks a question, accepts the learner's response, and provides feedback appropriate for the response. Since tutorial programs directly present instruction in addition to providing the opportunity for drill and practice, tutorial CBI is appropriate for the teaching of new knowledge and skills. Currently tutorial CBI lessons are available for most subjects at most levels. Tutorial CBI lessons are, however, more difficult to plan and develop than drill and practice CBI.

Simulation

Simulation CBI differs from both drill and practice CBI and tutorial CBI in that the interactions of the learners are not responses to questions but rather decisions they make in a role-playing situation. For example the

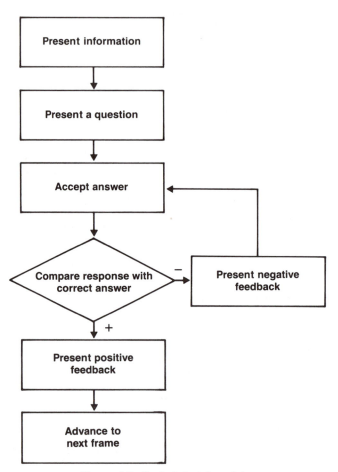

Figure 3.3. Basic tutorial model

learner may assume the role of a business manager and make decisions about how much of a product to produce and what price to charge. The learner could play the role of a member of Congress having to decide how to vote on certain legislation. In any case, a simulation is an attempt to develop a model of some aspect of reality and represent this in a computer program in such a way that learners can interact with it and receive feedback on their interactions. The logic for a simulation is shown in Figure 3.4.

Simulation CBI seeks to impart a higher level of understanding to the learners than is usually the case in drill and practice CBI or tutorial CBI.

Simulation Model

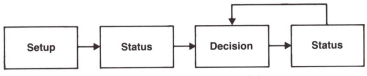

Figure 3.4. Simulation model

Simulations require the learners to apply rules and principles in lifelike situations. Simulation CBI is perhaps the most motivating of all CBI.

Alessi and Trollip (1985) divide simulation programs into four main categories: physical, procedural, situational, and process. Although there appears to be overlap among these categories, they provide a system for thinking about the different types of simulation programs. A physical simulation CBI lesson models some aspect of physical reality, such as an airplane's cockpit, with which the learner must interact.

Procedural simulations present a series of actions that constitute a particular procedure to be learned, such as medical diagnosis or electronic trouble-shooting.

Situational simulations represent human interactions with their environment or with other people. Examples of situational simulations include CBI programs that allow the student to retrace the route of explorers, planning and making decisions as the simulation proceeds.

Process simulations require the learners to establish an initial set of values for certain variables at the beginning of the simulation, then observe the process that occurs as a result of these values being carried out in the simulation. Process simulations allow learners to experiment with "what if" questions in a safe environment. For example, in a process simulation a learner may "play" with mixing different amounts of chemicals and observe the reaction, or the learner may see what would happen over a twenty-year period of saving different amounts of money. Simulations of any type can be effective ways of helping learners understand certain relationships or principles and how to apply them.

Other Possibilities

Although most CBI lessons can be classified into one of the three types—drill and practice, tutorial, and simulation—some CBI lessons have features of more than one type. For example a CBI simulation may include some tutorial instruction for the learner if he or she gets "lost" in the simulation and needs more direct instruction. More recently, variations on these three basic models have been developed, such as adaptive CBI models that adjust the content and instruction to fit different learners. In adaptive drill and practice CBI, the level of difficulty of the questions can be changed according to the learner's responses. If a learner is missing too many questions while proceeding through a drill and practice program, the program changes to easier questions. Likewise, if a learner is getting all or most questions right, the program selects more challenging questions. Adaptive tutorial models provide more examples or a more elaborate presentation to one learner than to another.

Some CBI models allow learners themselves more control over the lesson by giving them the option of seeing more examples, reading an overview of the content, changing to different content, taking a test, viewing an explanation of some concept, or using other such instructional activities. These models are called *learner-controlled* CBI. Adaptive and learner-controlled CBI models represent variations on the basic models.

Basic Principles of Organization

Regardless of the particular overall organization, every CBI lesson has a specific internal lesson structure based on either the content or the lesson's parts.

Various CBI tutorials with basically the same objectives—teaching parts of speech, for instance—may differ markedly both in terms of specific content and content sequence and in terms of the parts of the lesson. One program may be rich in examples, another lean; one may include a glossary of related terms, another may not. As a designer or selector of CBI software, your role is to assess the intended users and to find that program that will best fit their needs. If a lesson includes many vocabulary terms that are new to your students, you will want to make sure that the lesson you select includes a glossary. Also, if some of the students are unfamiliar with the content of the lesson, a glossary may be helpful. If, on the other hand, the lesson builds on familiar material and terms, obviously a glossary is less important.

Computer-based instruction allows considerable variation in the structure and content of lessons; there is no need for stale consistency in CBI lessons any more than there is a need for all textbooks to be exactly the same. Both the lesson's content and its treatment of the content may vary according to the intent and understanding of the lesson's authors.

TYPES OF INSTRUCTIONAL DISPLAYS

Several different types of instructional displays, or screens, are used in CBI lessons through which effective instructional principles are put into operation. The type of display that might be useful in a particular lesson depends on the nature of the lesson, the instructional content, and the audience. For ease of discussion, the different types of instructional displays are organized into three categories: preinstructional, instructional, and postinstructional.

- *Preinstructional displays* are those displays that a student views before receiving the new lesson content. They set the stage for the new learning.
- *Instructional displays* are those displays that present the new instructional content.
- *Postinstructional displays* are those displays that occur after the new instructional content has been presented.

Preinstructional Displays

Preinstructional displays serve to gain the learners' interest, focus their attention on the lesson, let learners know how the lesson is organized and what is expected from them, and assist learners in "calling up" previously learned material to which the new material can be related. This last function is particularly important.

The preinstructional display should include a statement of the instructional objectives that define the intent of the lesson. Like all efficient classroom lessons, CBI lessons must be introduced so that learners understand what is to follow. At a minimum, the learner should be shown the objectives for the lesson. The preinstructional display should also include an overview of the instructional content so that students can become familiar with the organization of the lesson. This is particularly true if the lesson presents a lot of new information. Students should be able to see how the lesson is organized so that they don't become "lost" in the specifics and never see the whole picture.

Effective CBI lessons also begin with a review of related material that is prerequisite to the material in the current lesson. Lessons should attempt to stimulate the students' prior knowledge. Successful learning builds on previously acquired knowledge (Ausubel, Novak, & Hanesian, 1978), and CBI lessons can reflect this principle by beginning with an *advance organizer,* an introductory passage designed to help the student recall the general area of knowledge to which the new material is related. *Examples* can show how the new content is related to previously learned content. A *pretest* might stimulate the student's recall of prior knowledge. Lessons might include *relational prompts* that specifically state the relationship between new content and previously acquired knowledge.

Other kinds of displays function well as preinstructional displays if they gain the student's attention, inform the student of the intent of the instruction, stimulate recall of related information, or assist the student in seeing the lesson's structure. One attention-gaining device is a *scenario* that relates to the content and demonstrates the need to know the new content. Scenarios should be used when the student's initial interest level is low or when he or she might not see the relevance of the content. A completed example might be used to show the student what he or she will be able to do when the lesson has been completed. A *review* or summary screen should be shown when the new knowledge builds directly on prior concepts, to stimulate recall of those concepts.

Instructional Displays

Instructional displays present new material, provide opportunity for practice, and guide the student in learning the new material. Displays should be designed to facilitate the acquisition of new knowledge. A variety of instructional displays can be used effectively in CBI lessons, depending on the instructional purpose, but each display must be understandable to the learner for whom it is intended. For example, the choice of vocabulary and examples must be based on an analysis of the intended learners so that it is appropriate. Language should be concise and clear. If the learner can't understand the instructional display, then he or she is not going to master the content of the lesson.

One common instructional display is a simple statement of the concept or rule. In a lesson on personal finance, for example, students might be told on a display screen that the daily compounding of interest means that each day the interest on a particular sum is computed and added to the previous balance. Similarly, in a CBI lesson on geometric figures, students can simply be told that a square is a geometric figure with four right angles and four equal sides. A simple statement of the concept or rule is helpful when the instructional objective is an intellectual skill, for example, mastery of a concept or rule, or problem solving.

Instructional displays often include *examples,* or *exemplars,* which illustrate the instructional content. In addition to defining a square, for instance, the CBI lesson on geometric figures might display examples of squares to help students acquire the concept of a square. Lessons frequently use *nonexamples,* or *negative exemplars,* in tandem with examples. Thus, in addition to showing geometric figures that are squares, the lesson might show figures that are not squares. Contrasting examples and nonexamples are essential in presenting material that involves discrimination or concept learning.

Instructional displays may often contain appropriately sequenced *elaborations* of new content. An initial screen may present the new concept at a broad or general level, and succeeding screens may contain more specific information about the concept. Finally the discussion may return to the more general level. This is what Reigeluth and Stein (1983) call the "zoom lens" approach. The CBI lesson first functions as a "wide-angle lens," taking in a panorama. Second, the lesson "zooms in" on one specific aspect of the content, presenting that aspect in detail. Third, the lesson returns to the wide angle to show that aspect in the broader context. Fourth, the lesson may zoom in again on a different aspect. And finally, the focus broadens again. These kinds of elaborations allow students both to understand the new material in its general context and to integrate the new information with previously acquired material. You should use or look for this kind of elaboration when the instructional objective is for students to acquire a considerable amount of new material. A simple fact or two can be acquired without elaboration. If you expect your students to learn the causes of World War II, however, you will probably want to use a program that includes elaboration displays. When learners must acquire considerable related information, elaboration is essential.

Postinstructional Displays

Effective learning requires activity beyond the presentation of new material. Postinstructional displays serve to reinforce or strengthen newly acquired knowledge. They also foster the retention of the new learning by aiding the retrieval process.

Several common displays are used in CBI lessons after new instruction has been presented. The most typical postinstructional display is an exercise, followed by appropriate feedback. After receiving new information from a CBI lesson, students are almost always required to practice using the new information by answering a series of questions or completing several problems that require its use. Effective lessons provide feedback regarding the accuracy of their answers so that students can confirm that they are correct or clear up any misconceptions if they are wrong. These exercises keep students actively engaged with the content and require them to apply what they have learned.

Exercises allow students to consolidate new learning. To be effective, they must provide appropriate feedback. If the student's answer is correct, the lesson should confirm that. If the answer is incorrect, the lesson should provide more elaborate feedback to identify the error and correct the student's misconceptions.

When a CBI lesson is carefully designed and organized, learners should successfully master most objectives. Exercises provide an opportunity for learners to experience that mastery. Exercises in some form should be included in all CBI lessons.

Some CBI lessons provide summaries as postinstructional displays to "refresh" the new learning. These summaries remind students of high-lights in the new content by again stressing the key points of the lesson. You should look for or include summaries in the lessons you select or design when the instructional objectives require learning a lot of new information.

Table 3.1 presents a summary of various types of instructional displays.

DESIGNING INSTRUCTIONAL DISPLAYS

How should these various types of instructional displays actually appear on the computer screen? There are several helpful points to consider when designing or assessing the design of a specific screen.

Screen Layout

The actual layout of an instructional screen should be clear, uncluttered, and consistent. The first thing to remember is that a computer display or screen is not a printed page. Each page in a book costs additional money to print; additional screens in a CBI program do not. There are, of course, storage limitations in all computers, but as long as your lesson is within the computer's capacity, using one hundred screens "costs" no more than using ten. It is neither necessary nor desirable, therefore, to fill every screen with text. Because it costs essentially the same to print a page in a book with one word on it or with a hundred words on it, book publishers fill each page with type. Designers of CBI programs, on the other hand, can keep their screens free of clutter by a liberal use of *white space,* which is the area of the screen that remains free of text. This white space improves the readability of screens and allows the student to focus more clearly and learn more than if a lesson had unnecessarily "busy" screens.

TABLE 3.1. TYPES OF INSTRUCTIONAL DISPLAYS

Preinstructional Displays	Instructional Displays	Postinstructional Displays
Instructional objectives	Statement of concepts/rules	Exercises
Content overview	Examples	Feedback
Advance organizer	Nonexamples	Summaries
Examples	Content elaborations	
Pretest		
Relational prompts		

Display screens should be consistent in format. There is nothing more disconcerting to students than a CBI program in which every screen looks different. Pick a screen layout, or a few screen layouts, and stick with them throughout the lesson. Just as a book does not use wide margins on one page and narrow margins on the next, or one size type and then another on succeeding pages of text, so too CBI screens should not employ inconsistent, and therefore confusing, layouts.

You may also want to use functional areas or *windows* in the lessons you design or select. A CBI designer can allocate certain aspects of the lesson to certain parts of the screen. For example, the directions to the student may always appear at the top of the screen; the instructional text may always appear on the left and examples on the right. On each screen, then, the student knows where to look for directions, explanations, and examples. Of course, you may not want all this material to appear on the screen at the same time. Nevertheless, it remains important to place material consistently and to have clean, uncluttered screens. They cost no more than the dreadful, messy ones, and they are much more pleasant to view and are much easier from which to learn.

Design of the Instructional Stimuli

It is one thing to provide information in writing about a topic; it is quite another to write instructional text. Text must communicate in such a way that the reader actually learns. Much has been written on learning from text, and much of this research applies to learning from text delivered through CBI (Hannum, 1986). A more complete description of desirable features in instructional text can be found in volumes edited by Jonassen (1982, 1985) and Duffy and Waller (1985).

In general, research supports the types of instructional displays mentioned earlier in this chapter. The text must be carefully organized, and the student must be made aware of this organization (Anderson & Armbruster, 1985). Tightly organized text seems to produce better learning results (Goetz and Armbruster, 1980). This kind of organization can be accomplished by the use of explicit statements about the lesson's structure, introductory and summary statements, and textual cues spread throughout the CBI lesson (Jonassen, 1985).

The instruction itself must be clear and understandable to the student, and new content should be illustrated with examples and nonexamples (Tennyson & Park, 1980), particularly for the learning of discriminations and concepts. Content should be made more concrete by the use of examples, analogies, metaphors, illustrations, and flowcharts (Carter, 1985). Analogies are particularly helpful when new material is completely unfamiliar to students; when the material requires discrimination or classification based on visual properties, such as classifying trees or rashes, an illustration is essential. Flowcharts should be used if the objective requires the student to follow a procedural sequence, such as solving a mathematical problem or performing a diagnosis. In all cases, transitions within the lesson should be made smoothly; cues should indicate when the topic is changing, or when any significant shift is made, such as going from discussion to summary.

The suggestions we have presented thus far for the design of instructional stimuli have described explicit ways to organize and present text. You may want to design or look for a program that allows students to generate their own text or images. Such generative activities facilitate the acquisition of new material by encouraging students to structure the new material themselves and to relate it to what they already know. Rather than providing a specific image to remember about the new material, a CBI lesson might elicit the student's own image of some aspect of the lesson's content. Instead of summarizing the content, the lesson might ask the user to develop his or her own summary. These generative activities actively engage students in processing the material they have just mastered (Jonassen, 1985; Pace, 1985).

Of course, CBI can consist of more than simply words on screens. Most computers are capable of a wide range of graphic representations. Such graphics, however, should be used cautiously. Graphics should convey instructional content and not simply adorn the screen. When graphic images do not add to the instructional message, they are superfluous and should be eliminated. Graphics can illustrate concepts or demonstrate relationships, but they should not be used simply as a change of pace or to "lighten up" the lesson.

Another option that is rapidly becoming feasible on many computers is synthesized speech, which can be used to present an auditory stimulus. This is obviously helpful in teaching a foreign language, but it may also be useful in other circumstances, such as in working with students with poor reading abilities. As with graphics, audio components in CBI lessons should serve some instructionally relevant purpose.

Directions to the Students

Students using CBI lessons should always know what is expected of them and how to proceed through the lesson. Directions to the student need to be clear and specific, and they need to appear at the point at which they are appropriate. If you are designing or selecting CBI, you should keep in mind three points about directions to students.

First, the directions for manipulating the computer or CBI lesson should be separate from the instructional content or text. For example, the directions should appear at the top or bottom of the screen, and they should do so consistently. Lessons might reserve one color for directions, not using that color for any other purpose. Directions can be set off from the text in a box or separate window.

Second, directions should appear at that point in the CBI program at which they are needed. Programs that begin with screen after screen of directions for everything in the lesson are rarely effective. After all, there are some limits to short-term memory! Most students will not remember directions given perhaps twenty minutes earlier that only now apply. Directions should appear where they are needed, not bunched up at the beginning of a lesson.

Third, directions must be understandable to students. Too often we encounter directions that could only be understood by someone who has already mastered the content, not by a student who is learning the material for the first time. Wording should be clear, simple, and free of jargon. Try the directions with a student or two to see whether they understand what is expected of them. Some provision for assistance or help should be built into the CBI lesson, and students should be able to access this help at any time, from any point in the lesson.

Learning Guidance

Often when students are learning new material, they can profit from assistance that is separate and apart from the subject matter itself. Several techniques can be used to provide this guidance. Cues and prompts can be placed in the CBI lesson to guide students, particularly when a response is required. Cues can provide assistance with the mechanics of making a response, as well as with the content on which the response is based. When students receive prompts for their responses, manipulation of the computer seems almost effortless. Students are encouraged to think about the instructional content and not waste time worrying about how to enter a response or manipulate the computer.

Another valuable way to provide learning guidance is through the use of *help screens* that the student can access at will. These help screens are a form of on-line documentation designed to assist the student when he or she becomes "stumped" while completing a CBI lesson. Help screens can be arranged to provide assistance with lesson content (a form of remedial help), or they can provide learning strategies (assistance in attacking the problem). Help screens might suggest, for instance, an approach to learning the material, a way to organize the material, or even some ways of remembering the material.

Learning guidance can also be provided by an attention focusing device that directs students to particular aspects of the lesson. Certain text might be highlighted, underlined, or printed in bold type. Color can bring attention to a word or phrase that is critical to the lesson. Perhaps the key word or phrase might be animated, so it moves across the screen for emphasis. Regardless of which technique is used, at times it is helpful to focus the students' attention during a CBI lesson. A summary of the points to look for in the design of instructional displays is presented in Table 3.2.

SUMMARY

In this chapter we have examined several aspects of designing, developing, and using CBI. We have explored the three main types of CBI—drill and practice, tutorial, and simulation. We have discussed the organization of CBI lessons—how lessons can be organized and how to communicate the organization to the students. We have described various types of instructional displays that could be used in CBI lessons. Creating effective CBI depends on these considerations. Selecting effective CBI lessons should be guided by these same considerations.

TABLE 3.2. DESIGNING INSTRUCTIONAL DISPLAYS

Screen Layout	Design of the Stimulus	Directions to Students	Learning Guidance
Much white space	Careful organization	Separate from instruction	Cues and prompts
Consistent format	Clear and understandable	Placed where needed	Help screens
Functional areas	Examples & nonexamples	Understandable	Attention-focusing devices
	Analogies & metaphors		
	Illustrations & flowcharts		
	Generative activities		
	Graphics		
	Synthesized speech		

PUTTING THE BOOK TO WORK

Read each of the following questions and review the source pages indicated. Respond to these questions, either in your mind or on paper. This process will provide a summary of the material presented in this chapter.

Question	*Source*
1. What are the general instructional design steps that should be followed in designing CBI?	36–38
2. What are the three basic types of CBI lessons? What are the characteristics of each?	38–41
3. Describe several preinstructional displays.	43–44
4. Describe several instructional displays.	44–45
5. Describe several postinstructional displays.	45–46
6. What are the characteristics of effective CBI screen displays?	46–47
7. What are some rules of thumb for the design of the instructional stimulus?	47–48
8. How can guidance be provided to the learner in CBI lessons?	49–50

CHAPTER 4

Instructional Management

Objectives

When you have read this chapter, you should be able to do the following:

1. Define computer-managed instruction and list the three types of CMI programs.
2. List five characteristics of a mastery learning approach to instruction and tell how CMI can facilitate each characteristic.
3. List five effective teaching principles and tell how CMI can facilitate each.
4. List the four components of a CMI program and define each.
5. Describe the components of a typical CMI curriculum setup.
6. Define integrated learning systems and give two examples in use today.
7. Define a generic CMI system and give two examples of generic programs in use today.
8. Define subject-specific CMI systems and give an example of a program in use today.
9. List and discuss at least three issues that should be addressed in selecting and implementing a CMI system.

INTRODUCTION: MANAGING INSTRUCTION WITH COMPUTERS

If there is any one use of computers in education that appears to be right in step with contemporary trends in the school reform movement, it is instructional management. North Carolina, Florida, California, Tennessee, and many other states have adopted legislation establishing "Basic Education Programs." Most of these programs specify a set of basic skill competencies that schools are to emphasize, to ensure that students are receiving an appropriate education. Many states have established statewide minimum competencies necessary to move from one grade level to another and to graduate. These efforts require fairly extensive individual student record-keeping systems. This is where computer-managed instruction (CMI) comes in.

When we hear the words *computer-managed instruction,* or *instructional management software,* we often assume that the topic is related to school administration and management. This association is wrong. Computer-managed instruction relates directly and specifically to the act of instruction. This chapter will discuss the use of instructional management software for the implementation of effective teaching principles, mastery learning, and individualized instructional procedures. *Computer-managed instruction* refers to the general process of storing, retrieving, analyzing, and reporting instructionally related information. Software programs designed to manage instructional information are frequently referred to as either *computer-managed instruction* (CMI) systems or *instructional management systems* (IMS). These software systems include the support of pupil record keeping, testing and test scoring, continuous progress monitoring, and progress reporting. A comprehensive CMI system allows the classroom teacher to keep a continuous progress record of each student's performance, based on a mastery learning or "diagnostic-prescriptive" approach to instruction.

Computer-based instructional management systems can be divided into three major categories: (1) integrated learning systems, (2) generic instructional management systems, and (3) subject-specific instructional management systems. *Integrated learning systems* (ILS) are the closest thing to a totally computer-based instructional system available. All steps in the common instructional cycle of assessment, diagnosis, instructional planning, instruction, and reassessment are implemented with the aid of computers. After a student signs on to the system for a specific subject, such as general mathematics, the computer selects and administers a pretest. Based on the computer-analyzed results of the test, the student's present level of objective mastery is determined, and the student is presented with the most appropriate tutorial lesson taken from a library of many lessons stored on the computer system. The ILS directs the student to interact with the tutorial program. At the end of the tutorial, another lesson is presented, based on the student's performance on the last lesson. A student can leave the program at any time and continue at the same point at the next session. The instructor can make a request at any time to the ILS system for individual or group progress or summary reports.

Generic instructional management systems are similar to the ILS, with two major exceptions. With these programs, the interactive instruction is not built into the system. Although students may receive computer-based instruction at times, the teacher is still responsible for the direct instruction for that subject. Another major difference is hinted at with the term *generic*. The users of generic systems can customize the program to manage any specific curriculum. The same system usually can manage a large number of different subjects. For example, if a school's staff members have developed their own series of instructional objectives for each of the basic skill areas, they can set up the generic system to conduct instructional management tasks for their curriculum objectives in each basic skills subject area. Because generic instructional management systems focus on the instructional management and not on computer-based instruction, they usually provide more comprehensive record-keeping functions and a wider array of available reports.

As the name implies, *subject-specific instructional management systems* are instructional management systems that have been developed to support a specific subject and curriculum. Therefore, a major difference between this type of CMI program and a generic CMI system is that the subject-specific program comes with the subskills, instructional objectives, test questions, and instructional resources already set up in the computer software program. The most common examples of these types of CMI systems are programs developed to correlate with basal reading and mathematics textbook series sold by large publishing companies. Although a few of these programs allow the user to make changes in some areas of the setup, such as adding or deleting instructional objectives in the system, most will not allow changes in the curriculum.

PROMOTING EFFECTIVE SCHOOLS THROUGH COMPUTER-MANAGED INSTRUCTION

Many people believe that the use of computers for instructional management holds more potential for positive impact in the schools than any other use (Baker, 1978). In comparison to the attention received by computer-assisted instruction (CAI), that is, using a computer for direct instruction, CMI has received very little attention from educators. This relative lack of interest is puzzling, in view of the potential benefits that can be gained with the use of computer technology for this purpose. As mentioned in Chapter 1, Kulik and his colleagues conducted a meta-analysis of forty-five studies on the effectiveness of computer-based instruction (Kulik, Bangert, & Williams, 1984). They reviewed CMI research as well as CAI research and found that the use of a CMI system contributed as much as, if not more than, CAI to achievement gains of students using computer-based instruction.

Although American educators acknowledge that individual learners differ in regard to instructional content, learning style, and learning speed, instructional practice continues to put students into large groups for instruction, teaching all students the same content at the same pace. The result is that individual differences are only superficially met, and then only when the need for varying the curriculum is very apparent—such as in establishing special individualized instructional programs for exceptional children.

The demands on the instructor's time in dealing with the additional monitoring and paperwork are multidimensional. Noninstructional teacher tasks involved in individual mastery learning include developing, administering, and scoring tests; analyzing test results; and writing and updating instructional plans with mastered and projected instructional objectives. All these tasks repeated for the approximately thirty pupils an elementary teacher is responsible for make it obvious that using an individual instructional process is next to impossible. Yet it is exactly these time-consuming management tasks in which a computer excels.

Computer-Managed Instruction and Mastery Learning

One approach to individual instruction has been mastery learning, as developed by Bloom and his colleagues (Bloom, 1971). Mastery learning requires a student to demonstrate a specific skill before proceeding to another skill or set of skills. Each student works at his or her own pace. At regularly scheduled times, or when the student feels ready, he or she takes a test to determine whether or not the skill or skills have been learned. The tests provide feedback to students and help the teacher plan for subsequent lessons and instructional activities for each student. Students who do not achieve mastery, as indicated by the test results, continue to work on those skills through additional and sometimes alternative activities.

The effectiveness of the mastery learning approach to instruction is well documented. When students are taught with mastery learning techniques, they demonstrate greater gains in achievement than when they are taught with traditional instruction (Chandler, 1982; Human & Cohen, 1979). Equally convincing evidence indicates that mastery learning techniques also result in important gains in affective learning

(Block, 1972; Dunkleberger & Knight, 1977). As suggested by Heikkinen and Dunkleberger (1985), there is widespread support among investigators of instructional effectiveness for the superiority of mastery learning techniques over traditional teaching methods.

John B. Carroll's (1963) benchmark work on the relationship between time and learning, and subsequent studies by Benjamin Bloom and his colleagues (Block, 1971; Block & Anderson, 1975; Bloom, 1974; Bloom, 1976) documenting the effectiveness of mastery learning, have provided a foundation for shaping effective teaching practices, particularly with handicapped students. These data strongly support the superiority of mastery learning over conventional instructional practices. The evidence is so convincing that some researchers suggest that documentation of effective implementation of mastery learning procedures can be used as a de facto representation of achievement.

Mastery learning practices include (1) frequent student testing and feedback to establish the current level of objective mastery, (2) a clear identification of skill expectations (instructional objectives) and learning tasks for each student, (3) an increase in the amount of time each student spends on instructional tasks, (4) prescriptive instruction geared toward the mastery of specific skills or objectives, and (5) objective mastery record keeping (Block, 1971).

The Adaptive Learning Environments Model (ALEM), a project concerning special education students in the New York City Schools, conducted a quantitative synthesis of a large number of research studies conducted over a ten-year period. Their review indicated that effective instruction included the following characteristics:

- Students work at their own pace.
- Student abilities are tested/monitored frequently.
- Instruction is based on the assessed abilities of each student.
- Teachers, students, and parents receive frequent reports of mastery.

Implementation of the model instructional program resulted in a significantly higher level of achievement of the students involved. The ALEM project included the use of an instructional management system, designed to maximize the use of available classroom and school resources such as students' and teachers' time (Wang, Rubenstein, & Reynolds, 1985).

As discussed earlier, one of the biggest problems encountered in implementing mastery learning programs has been the management of the increased amount of testing, record keeping, and reporting. Through the use of the information and data-processing capabilities of computers, the ALEM project was able to minimize the negative effects of these labor-intensive instructional activities. In support of using microcomputers for the management of test information, McCune (1982) points out the growing importance of assessment and evaluation in responding to the need for more accountability in our schools. She cites the trends toward greater emphasis on individual testing—standardized testing and criterion reference testing, timely feedback of test results, and broader applications of testing. Killian (1983) suggests that the only way schools are going to be able to handle the increased workload related to testing and monitoring students' progress is through use of computer technology.

Since the 1981–1982 school year, the Pittsburgh Public schools have developed and implemented the Monitoring and Achievement in Pittsburgh (MAP) Project. Similar to the practices just discussed, components of the MAP Project include the indentification of skill expectations, focused instruction, monitoring of achievements, appropriate instructional resources, time on task, and staff development. Since the introduction of the MAP Project in 1980, the Pittsburgh Public Schools report that levels of student achievement have improved markedly. They credit the MAP Project for these gains (School District of Pittsburgh, 1985).

Computer-Managed Instruction and Research on Effective Schools

To assist public schools in their school improvement efforts, the U.S. Department of Education (1986) summarized the effective schools research (discussed in chapter 2) in a publication entitled *What Works: Research About Teaching and Learning*. Initial reactions to *What Works* have been mixed. To some, these recommendations represent the federal government's intrusion into establishing public school curriculum policy, a sensitive issue in American education. Most informed educators would agree, however, that the principles presented in *What Works* are indeed supported by substantial educational research evidence. Table 4.1 presents the positive relationships between many of the effective teaching principles and the use of a computer-managed instructional program in support of mastery learning.

COMPONENTS OF COMPREHENSIVE COMPUTER-MANAGED INSTRUCTIONAL PROGRAMS

One of the biggest differences in CMI software systems relates to the level of comprehensiveness of the systems. The three major types of CMI systems mentioned previously—integrated learning systems, generic

**TABLE 4.1. RELATIONSHIP BETWEEN EFFECTIVE SCHOOLS RESEARCH
AND THE USE OF COMPUTER-BASED INSTRUCTIONAL MANAGEMENT SYSTEMS**

Principle	Applications
Teachers who set clear expectations of what is to be learned obtain greater academic performance from their students.	Once instructional objectives are established and entered into the software system, reports listing the objectives for each individual student can be quickly generated. Objective mastery reports can be shared with students and their parents as a continuous reminder of the expectations for each course of study. Based on up-to-date objective mastery information, teachers can plan daily and weekly instructional activities around each student's objectives.
When teachers explain exactly what students are expected to learn, and demonstrate the steps to accomplish a particular academic task, students learn more.	
When instruction is geared toward mastery of specific academic skills or objectives, students learn more.	
Frequent and systematic monitoring of students' progress helps students, parents, teachers, administrators, and policymakers identify strengths and weaknesses in learning instruction.	Once tests are entered into the software, they can be easily administered, scored, and analyzed. Based on the results of testing, individual pupil objective mastery files are updated, and new reports can be generated to provide feedback to each student. This structured, objective based approach to instruction has been proven to be very effective for teaching basic skills.
The most important characteristics of effective schools are strong instructional leadership, a safe and orderly climate, school-wide emphasis on basic skills, high teacher expectations for student achievement, and continuous assessment of pupil progress.	

instructional management systems, and subject-specific instructional management systems—represent categories of comprehensiveness of the system. Many instructional management software systems, particularly those published and/or sold by textbook publishers, have been developed to be used with specific curriculum programs. For example, Computer Curriculum Corporation (1983), founded by Patrick Suppes, has developed an integrated learning system that includes not only computer-managed instruction but also computer-based tutorial lessons that are diagnostically linked to the computer-managed instructional components of the system. The term *integrated learning system* refers to the most comprehensive systems, which theoretically contain all the elements of the instructional cycle.

The Microcomputer Instructional Management System (MIMS), published by CBT/McGraw-Hill (1984) is designed to be used with specific instructional, testing, and scoring products published by CBT/McGraw-Hill. The MIMS program is an example of a subject-specific instructional management system. Other instructional management software programs allow users to establish and use their own instructional objectives, test items, and instructional prescriptions. These programs usually devote a component of their program to a series of functions that allow the user to add objectives, test questions, and instructional prescriptions. This component usually resembles a word-editing or word-processing program.

Although there are a number of variations in the major components of instructional management software systems, most comprehensive programs include the components that are illustrated in Figure 4.1, Computer-Managed Instructional System Flowchart. Each of the components in the flowchart is discussed here.

Electronic Storage of Curricular Scope and Sequence

A computer-managed instructional system should be flexible enough to allow the addition of a curricular scope and sequence developed by the user (agency staff) and/or one already entered into the CMI program. The specific curricular information that has been, or is to be, entered into a computer-managed instructional program is frequently referred to as the setup. Typically, the curriculum setup for a subject will include (1) a set of subskills, (2) instructional objectives for each subskill, (3) criterion reference test questions correlated with each objective, and (4) instructional strategies and materials correlated to each objective. Although the general concepts of subskills, instructional objectives, criterion referenced questions, and teaching prescriptions are well known to most educators, it is important to comment on each of these in relationship to their use in computer-managed instructional software systems.

Subject Subskills. A prerequisite for use of a computer-managed instructional system is the adoption of a mastery learning philosophy of instruction. Ample evidence is provided in chapter 2 and in this chapter to support the effectiveness of a mastery learning approach to instruction. To facilitate the use of mastery learning, skills to be learned are classified, or divided, into logical subskill categories. Subskill categories contain a cluster of abilities highly related to one another. Ideally, these positive relationships will be supported by empirical evidence from the research literature on the subject. In the absence of empirical evidence, a construct validity is often the foundation for the delineation of subskill categories.

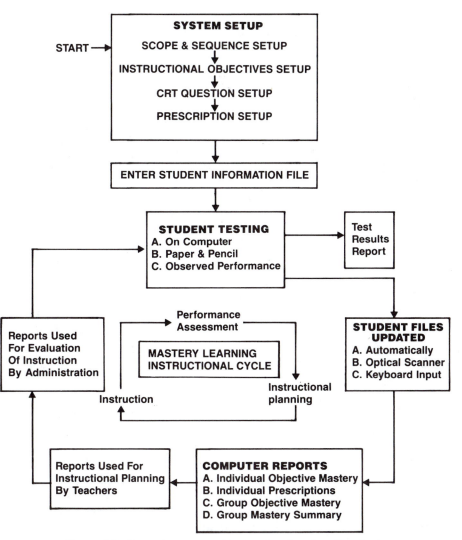

Figure 4.1. Computer-managed instructional system flowchart

For example, upon examination of five widely used American history textbooks, you may find that the content is divided across periods of time. Hence, one logical organization of subskill categories for American history might include the Discovery Period, Revolutionary War Period, Exploration and Expansion Period, Civil War Period, Industrial Growth Period, and Twentieth Century. Figure 4.2 displays a typical CMI setup that includes examples of the use of subskills.

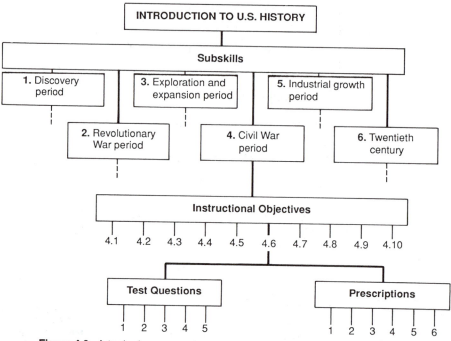

Figure 4.2. A typical scope and sequence setup for an Instructional Management System

Instructional Objectives. It is rare to find an educator who has not attended a number of lectures or workshops on the topic of writing instructional objectives. Although the concept of developing and using instructional objectives is widely accepted in U.S. education, the application, or use of instructional objectives in the instructional process, varies widely. The use of instructional management software does not dictate a particular approach to writing instructional objectives. They can be quite vague, such as "to increase the student's ability to recognize commonly used words at the second-grade level." Or they can be very specific: "By June 1, 1990, when one-syllable words with a final consonant sound are pronounced by the teacher, the student will correctly identify the final consonant in each word nine out of ten times." Most CMI software systems will have a limit on the length of each objective. Length limitations are usually a function of the type and size of the computer operating the CMI system. Also, ten-page reports are not as likely to be read as thoroughly as are two-page reports, and they take up more file space. Another point to consider when developing instructional objectives to use with a CMI software system is that the criterion for mastery of an objective will be directly tied to the test questions linked with the objective. Therefore, criteria statements in the instructional objective itself do not have to be explicit. In fact many CMI software programs use specific ability descriptions (e.g., combine simple words to form a compound word) instead of specifically stated instructional objectives.

Test Questions. Test questions are used to determine mastery of a particular objective. There are a number of acceptable procedures for determining the presence or absence of a specific skill, such as the use of structured observations of pupil behavior or pupil products. The use of paper-and-pencil testing has traditionally been the most widely used form of measuring mastery of basic skills content in the public schools. Most basic skills objectives can be measured adequately through the use of objective, criterion referenced tests. Higher-order objectives, however, are best measured through observation, essay-type questions, and evaluating student products. Though current computer-based testing procedures are not very helpful in determining mastery of higher-order objectives involving analysis, synthesis, evaluation, or cognitive strategies (as discussed in chapter 1), the use of objective tests is on the rise across all levels of organized education.

Test questions and corresponding test keys are entered into the instructional management software system through a setup process that is much like using a word-processing program. A test key can be set up for any objective test, whether it is a well-known standardized test, such as the California Achievement Test (CBT/McGraw-Hill, 1985), or a locally used teacher-made criterion referenced test. When establishing a test key, most CMI programs will require identification of each question number, the correct response for each question, and the related instructional objective for each question. If test items are being developed to be entered into a CMI software system, to be printed by the computer or to be administered on the computer, there will be some guidelines to follow. Most CMI programs will have limits on the type of question (e.g., multiple choice), length of question, length of possible answer choices, number of questions used to measure mastery of a particular objective, number of possible answer choices per question, and total length of the test.

Good test questions should be valid and reliable and are not easy to develop. The goal in developing the test questions to be used in mastery learning instruction is to create items that will clearly measure whether or not a pupil has mastered a particular objective or skill. Some CMI programs include the capability to conduct an item analysis on tests that are administered as part of the CMI process. These programs are extremely helpful in determining which items are satisfactory in discriminating between students who have mastered a particular objective and students who have not. The item analysis process and software programs that conduct item analyses will be discussed in more detail in chapter 5.

Teaching Prescriptions. Most CMI programs provide a "prescriptions" feature. Prescriptions in CMI programs, as well as in many other types of educational practice, refer to instructional strategies, activities, materials, or other resources that can be used by a teacher, tutor, or student in working toward achievement of a particular instructional objective. To this end, prescriptions are developed for each objective and entered into the CMI program, using the setup or editing features of the program. Although *prescriptions* is used when describing this function of CMI programs, it is an overgeneralized use of the term. In medicine, for example, prescriptions are developed to deal with underlying causes of a problem rather than the symptoms. In this application, however, prescriptions refers to instructional activities and/or materials. The prescriptions may be the same for any student working on a specific instructional objective. There have been a few attempts at developing CMI programs that diagnose learning styles or information-processing strengths and weaknesses. However, there is meager evidence supporting the effectiveness of instructional techniques that diagnose learning styles and/or processing abilities. With some CMI programs, prescriptions come already prepared and entered by the publisher. Other CMI software programs allow the users to develop and enter their own prescriptions.

Electronic Storage of Individual Student Files and Records

A central function of any CMI software program is the storage and retrieval of instructional information about individual students. The CMI programs vary widely in terms of the capabilities available. Menus are usually available within the program to establish student lists. The extent to which background and enrollment information about individual students can be stored and retrieved in various forms depends on the configuration and power of the computer system in use, as well as the software program in use. When establishing a student or class list, most programs will request the entry of such information as the student's name, identification number, age, grade, and teacher. More elaborate programs may ask for additional background information, such as parents' name and address, student's advisor, sex of student, race of student, and class section as well as class.

Once a student file is established, test and achievement data will automatically be written into that file whenever a test is scored for that student or when a teacher wishes to enter achievement information into the file directly. Individual reports, various group reports, and summary reports are derived from the information found in the student files at the time of the report.

Testing, Scoring, and Interpretation

Although programming techniques are emerging that allow the computer to make judgments about essays or fill-in-the blank responses to questions (see chapter 5), most computer testing systems only accommodate multiple-choice and/or true-or-false questions. This restriction is similar to those encountered when using a standardized test such as the California Achievement Test (CBT/McGraw-Hill, 1985), where the pupil records his or her responses on an optical scanning sheet. There are at least three methods of test administration in relationship to the use of computer-managed instructional programs.

The first method has pupils taking tests in the traditional manner. The test is printed on paper, and the pupil, using a pencil, indicates his or her response to each question on the test itself. After the test is completed, a staff member enters into the computer the answers indicated by each pupil, using a keyboard entry screen in the CMI program. Once the test results for a particular student are entered, the CMI program automatically scores the test and updates the student's objective mastery file.

The second method of test administration requires additional equipment, an optical scanning device that is attached to the computer hosting the CMI program. The pupil records his or her answers onto an optical scanning sheet designed to be used with the CMI program. After the test is completed, a staff member feeds the optical scanning sheets through the scanner, and the CMI program automatically scores the test and updates the student's objective mastery file.

The third method calls for the pupil to take the test *on line,* or on a computer. In this case the test questions reside in memory files in the computer. After the pupil identifies himself or herself and indicates which test is to be taken, the test items appear on the monitor screen one at a time. The pupil selects a response for each question and moves on to the next question until the test is completed. No paper-and-pencil testing is necessary.

The advantages and disadvantages of each of these methods are fairly obvious. The first method is more time consuming and tedious, although it does eliminate the teacher time devoted to the scoring and interpretation of the tests. In the second procedure, use of a scanner requires the purchase of a scanner and, initially, the presence of additional technical expertise in ensuring that the scanning process is running reliably. The third method requires either a network of multiple computer terminals or microcomputers or pupils taking the test at a "stand alone" unit, one at a time. Each of these options has advantages and disadvantages in terms of equipment availability, complexity, costs, and logistics of pupil test taking.

Several testing options are available to the teacher once the tests, or more accurately the test keys, have been created. Students can take multiple-choice tests on the computer, or a specific test can be printed to be taken in the traditional paper-and-pencil fashion. After the test is taken, the teacher can enter the results for each student into the computer. The IMS program will score the results of the test and, based on a criterion level selected by the teacher, update the objective mastery file of the student.

Instructional Management Reports

Most CMI software programs produce several very useful reports. Individual and group reports indicating progress of students can be printed to assist with instructional planning, parent reporting, and program evaluation. Individual mastery reports usually provide several options: (1) a chart of all the objectives in the curriculum area, indicating which objectives have been mastered, which objectives are projected (or being worked on currently), and which objectives are not applicable; (2) a list of the objectives mastered and objectives projected; and (3) a list of instructional materials or activities recommended for each objective. (See Figure 4.3, pages 67–70.)

In addition, many programs will provide group objective mastery reports and group summary reports. Group objective mastery reports are useful to instructors in making decisions for grouping students for instruction based on each student's objectives. Group summary reports indicate the percentage of students mastering each objective in a particular group, class, or school. Figure 4.4, pages 71–74 shows examples of different kinds of reports produced on IMS.

Most CMI programs will also print the current status of the various files in the system, providing student lists, lists of instructional objectives, prescription lists, and lists of test questions.

COMPUTER-MANAGED INSTRUCTIONAL SYSTEMS IN USE

There has been a continuous increase in the number of CMI programs in use in educational agencies during the last several years. Many of these programs have been developed for commercial purposes. Others have

Figure 4.3a. Scope and Sequence Chart from an Objective Mastery Report produced by an IMS System

Oak Grove Elementary School

OBJECTIVES MASTERY REPORT

Name: William Cummings　　　　　　Today's date: 01-15-88
Age: 12　　　　　　　　　　　　　　　Grade: 6
Teacher: Cobbie　　　　　　　　　　School: Oak Grove Elementary School

Word Ident.		Comprehension		Study & Research		Literary U & A	
		RC.21					
		RC.20	01-01-80				
		RC.19	01-01-80				
		RC.18					
		RC.17					
		RC.16					
		RC.15					
		RC.14					
		RC.13					
		RC.12	P				
		RC.11	01-23-87				
		RC.10					
WI.9	01-23-87	RC.9		SR.9	01-01-80		
WI.8	01-23-87	RC.8	P	SR.8	P		
WI.7		RC.7	P	SR.7			
WI.6		RC.6	01-23-87	SR.6	01-01-80	LU.6	01-01-80
WI.5		RC.5	P	SR.5	P	LU.5	01-01-80
WI.4		RC.4	P	SR.4	01-23-87	LU.4	
WI.3	01-23-87	RC.3	P	SR.3	12-01-86	LU.3	P
WI.2		RC.2	P	SR.2	P	LU.2	01-01-80
WI.1	01-23-87	RC.1	01-23-87	SR.1	P	LU.1	P

LANGUAGE ARTS—'P': Mastery Projected　　　'MM-DD-YY': Date Mastered

Oak Grove Elementary School
OBJECTIVES MASTERY REPORT

Name: William Cummings   Today's date: 01-15-88

LANGUAGE ARTS OBJECTIVES—MASTERED

WI.1	Uses phonics: consonants
WI.3	Uses word structure: root words
WI.8	Uses word structure: compounds
WI.9	Uses word structure: contractions
RC.1	Understands words/phrases/sentences: pronouns/adverbs
RC.6	Understands words/phrases/sentences: connotations
RC.11	Understands paragraphs: recognizes place relationships
RC.19	Makes judgments: draws conclusions
RC.20	Makes judgments: distinguishes between fact and opinion
SR.3	Locates/interprets information in reference sources: beginning skills
SR.4	Locates/interprets information in reference sources: intermediate skills
SR.6	Organizes information
SR.9	Locates/interprets standard book features: advanced skills
LU.2	Recognizes types of literature: autobiography and biography
LU.5	Recognizes/appreciates techniques and elements of style: personification
LU.6	Recognizes/appreciates techniques and elements of style: point of view

Figure 4.3b. A List of Objectives Mastered from an Objective Mastery Report produced by an IMS System

been developed as a result of a specific software need and used primarily in one agency. In this section, a number of examples are given of CMI systems in use. These descriptions are divided across the categories of CMI programs discussed earlier in this chapter: (1) integrated learning systems, (2) generic instructional management systems, and (3) subject-specific instructional management systems. Each example presents the hardware and software characteristics, the power and capacities of the program, and the way in which the system is used.

Integrated Learning Systems

Integrated learning systems (ILS) are software systems that provide comprehensive computer-based instructional lessons that include a computer-based instructional management system. Most ILS software systems have been developed to run on specific computer systems that have large amounts of storage capacity. As indicated earlier, the main difference between this category of CMI and the other categories is that

Oak Grove Elementary School

OBJECTIVES MASTERY REPORT

Name: William Cummings   Today's date: 01-15-88

LANGUAGE ARTS OBJECTIVES—PROJECTED

RC.2	Understands words/phrases/sentences: similes and metaphors
RC.3	Understands words/phrases/sentences: appropriate word meaning
RC.4	Understands words/phrases/sentences: unfamiliar words
RC.5	Understands words/phrases/sentences: idioms
RC.7	Understands words/phrases/sentences: prefixes/suffixes
RC.8	Understands paragraphs: recognizes main idea and supporting details
RC.12	Understands paragraphs: recognizes time relationships
SR.1	Uses basic location aids: index
SR.2	Locates/interprets standard book features
SR.5	Evaluates information and sources
SR.8	Uses basic location aids: advanced indexing
LU.1	Identifies story elements
LU.3	Recognizes types of literature: historical fiction, myth, legend, science fiction, and tall tale

Figure 4.3c. A List of Projected Objectives from an Objective Mastery Report produced by an IMS System

integrated learning systems provide tutorial instruction as well as instructional management. Most other CMI systems are designed for instructional management but are not automatically linked to computer-based tutorial programs. The traditional emphasis of ILS software has been on basic skills of reading and mathematics. Typically, an ILS system begins with diagnostic or placement testing on the computer. Based on the student's performance, an initial level of instruction is determined and tutorial lessons are presented in sequence. As the student interacts with the tutorial program, responses are judged and a record of his or her performance and progress is kept by the computer. At the end of a lesson, unit, or module, a performance test is administered. The student's objective mastery file is then updated based on his or her performance. Most ILS programs allow the student to discontinue a session with the computer at any time. The next time the student signs on to the ILS system, he or she will begin at the spot at which the lesson was discontinued.

Computer Curriculum Corporation's Microhost Instructional System. The Microhost system (Computer Curriculum Corporation, 1983) is used in over 1,300 elementary, secondary, and adult educational pro-

Figure 4.3d. Suggested Instructional Activities from an Objective Mastery Report produced by an IMS System

Oak Grove Elementary School

OBJECTIVES MASTERY REPORT

Name: William Cummings   Today's date: 01-15-88

LANGUAGE ARTS PRESCRIPTIONS—PROJECTED

RC.7:

Make a list of affixes on a piece of paper. Some affixes you might use are
re-, un-, -ly, -er, and -est.

On small pieces of paper, write several root words to which prefixes can be
added, for example: play, happy, easy, paint, slow.

Ask your child to select a piece of paper with a root word on it and choose an
appropriate prefix or suffix to add to that word.

RC.8:

Read your child a series of short stories. Ask him or her to give you another
title for the story. You can ask questions like:
"What would be another good name for this story?"
"What else could we call this story?"

After you have finished watching a television story, ask your child to tell you
what might happen to the main character in the future.

Read a story with your child. When the story is finished, ask your child
questions about the story. For example:
"What happened first?" "When did _____ happen?" "What
happened in the first, middle, or last part of the story?"

RC.12:

Read stories to your child about different time periods. Help your child
recognize descriptions of setting, dress, language, and actions that relate
to different time periods. Ask your child to identify the time period for
each story.

Take your child to visit at least one older neighbor or family member. Ask this
person to describe his or her earlier life. Show your child old photographs
and point out how things were different then. Then show some recent
photographs. Help your child relate these facts to past and present time.

Ask your child to select a time period and to make a collection of pictures that
show aspects of that time period.

Ask your child to use details in the pictures and tell you a story about that time
period.

Figure 4.4a. An example of a Student List/Roll produced by an IMS system

Oak Grove Elementary School

STUDENT LIST

ID CODE	STUDENT	AGE	GRADE	TEACHER
677722	Allison, Donald	12	6	Cobbie
561233	Aquireie, Linda	8	3	James
53212	Atkins, Kathy	8	3	James
557877	Attenbury, Melvin	9	3	James
988777	Atwater, Karra	12	6	Harmon
983472	Baccurak, Bruce	8	3	James
543992	Ballemy, Mary	10	4	Wilson
343999	Bannister, Stacy	9	4	Wilson
653972	Bennington, Jerry	12	6	Harmon
783333	Benson, Lee	13	6	Harmon
530012	Berstien, Connie	9	4	Wilson
763000	Birrenson, Hope	12	6	Cobbie
783339	Boatman, Rhonda	9	4	Wilson
876292	Buford, Marnie	12	6	Cobbie
674621	Cannon, Samuel	13	6	Knight
799332	Cappenter, Evie	7	3	James
632992	Chamers, Monica	13	6	Knight
755912	Chitendon, Calvin	12	6	Cobbie
771182	Criston, Steve	12	6	Harmon
780032	Croft, Kattie	11	6	Knight
785800	Cummings, William	11	6	Cobbie
721991	Eckardson, Vera	12	6	Harmon
710102	Edson, Dennis	12	6	Harmon
653220	Edwards, Lewis	13	6	Harmon
719991	Farris, Kinnard	9	4	Wilson
623992	Framington, Tom	9	4	Wilson
711188	Framinson, Elie	8	4	Wilson
766266	Frirson, Rick	12	6	Cobbie
527476	Gephart, James	8	4	Wilson
633663	Gobble, Steven	8	3	James
722304	Golden, Morris	9	3	James
499912	Goodlad, Gary	12	6	Harmon
654844	Green, Ann	12	6	Harmon
299223	Gregson, Marcus	12	6	Harmon
700210	Harborson, Gregg	11	6	Knight
521212	Harcout, Rita	12	6	Cobbie
923657	Harrison, Talbot	8	3	James
433610	Heneke, Lyle	12	6	Knight
612663	Hopkins, Charles	11	6	Cobbie
553400	Jameson, Lisa	13	6	Cobbie
440210	Jennings, Alice	8	3	James

Figure 4.4b. An example of a Group Objective Mastery Report produced by an IMS system

Oak Grove Elementary School

GROUP MASTERY REPORT—Comprehension

Group: Cobbie's Sixth-Grade Class   Today's date: 01-15-88

* = MASTERED   P = PROJECTED

Column headers (R = objective row, C = comprehension objective), numbered RC1–RC21:

Name	1	2	3	4	5	6	7	8	9	10	11	12	13	14	15	16	17	18	19	20	21
Allison, Donald	*	P	P	P	P	P	P	P			*	*									
Atwater, Karra	*	P	*	*	*	*	*	P			*	P									
Bennington, Jerry	*	*	*	P	P	*	*	P			P	*				*	*				
Benson, Lee	*	*	*	*	*	*	*	P			P	*				*	*				
Birrenson, Hope	*	*	*	*	*	*	*	P			*	*				*	*				
Buford, Marnie	*	P	*	*	*	*	*	P			*	P				*	*				
Cannon, Samuel	*	P	*	*	*	*	*	*			P	*				*	*				
Chamers, Monica	*	P	*	*	*	*	P	P			P	*				P	*				
Chitendon, Calvin	*	*	*	P	*	*	*	P			*	*				*	*				
Criston, Steve	*	*	*	*	*	P	*	*			*	*				P	P				
Croft, Kattie	*	*	*	*	*	*	*	*			*	*				*	*				
Cummings, William	*	P	P	P	P	*	P	P			*	P				*	*				
Eckardson, Vera	*	*	P	*	*	*	P	*			*	P				*	*				
Edson, Dennis																					
Edwards, Lewis	*	*	P	*	P	*	*	P			*	*									
Frirson, Rick	*	P	*	P	*	*	*	*			*	*				*	*				
Goodlad, Gary																					
Green, Ann	*	P	*	*	P	P	P	*			*	P				*	P				
Gregson, Marcus	*	P	*	*	*	*	*	P			*	*				P	P		P	P	
Harborson, Gregg	*	P	*	*	*	*	*	*			*	P									
Harcout, Rita	P	*	*	P	P	P	*	P			P	*									
Heneke, Lyle	*	*	*	*	*	*	*	P			*	*				*	*				
Hopkins, Charles	*	*	*	*	*	*	*	P			P	P				P	*				
Jameson, Lisa	*	P	*	*	P	*	P	P			*	*				*	*				
Jillian, Tracy	*	P	*	*	*	*	*	*			*	*				*	P				
Johnson, Allen																					
Kapperman, Sally	*	*	*	*	*	*	*	P			*	*				P	*				
Kinsear, Helen	*	*	*	*	*	*	P	*			*	*				*	*				
Kossenter, Stan	*	*	P	*	P	*	*	P			P	*				*	*				
Kukla, Jerry																					
Lainnear, Anne																					
Laney Jr, Larry E.	P	P	P	P	P	P	*	*			P	P				P	*				
Langly, Jennie	*	P	*	*	*	*	P	*			*	*				*	*				
Lee, Jerome	*	*	*	*	*	*	*	*			*	*				*	*				
Lowenstien, Lila	*	*	*	*		*					*					*	*				

72

Figure 4.4c. An example of a Summary of Objective Mastery produced by an IMS system

Oak Grove Elementary School

GROUP SUMMARY MASTERY REPORT—Comprehension

Group: Cobbie's Sixth-Grade Class Today's date: 01-15-88

	RC.1		RC.2		RC.3		RC.4		RC.5		RC.6		RC.7		RC.8	
	No.	%	No.	%	No.	%	No.	%	No.	%	No.	%	No.	%	No.	%
Mastered	36	78	23	50	29	63	32	69	30	65	31	67	31	67	14	30
Projected	2	4	16	34	10	21	7	15	9	19	7	15	8	17	24	52
N/A	8	17	7	15	7	15	7	15	7	15	8	17	7	15	8	17

	RC.9		RC.10		RC.11		RC.12		RC.13		RC.14		RC.15		RC.16	
	No.	%	No.	%	No.	%	No.	%	No.	%	No.	%	No.	%	No.	%
Mastered	0	0	0	0	28	60	27	58	0	0	0	0	0	0	0	0
Projected	0	0	0	0	10	21	12	26	0	0	0	0	0	0	1	2
N/A	46	100	46	100	8	17	7	15	46	100	46	100	46	100	45	97

	RC.17		RC.18		RC.19		RC.20		RC.21	
	No.	%	No.	%	No.	%	No.	%	No.	%
Mastered	0	0	0	0	29	63	30	65	0	0
Projected	1	2	0	0	6	13	5	10	0	0
N/A	45	97	46	100	11	23	11	23	46	100

grams. This system uses its own minicomputer, which is linked to Microhost microcomputer terminals or to Atari ST microcomputers. The system can handle up to 128 terminals, with at least one printer for every sixteen terminals. The Microhost system is also compatible with the Atari ST microcomputer terminals with 512K memory, distributive processing, and color high-resolution graphics. The software programs run with a Unix-operating system.

Computer Curriculum Corporation has one of the most extensive libraries of courseware available to run on its ILS system, offering about thirty courses totaling more than 2,500 hours of instruction time. The bulk of this courseware is in the subject areas of mathematics, reading, language arts, and computer education. The CCC system provides several different types of instructional reports, including individual ability levels by skill and course, group weaknesses, individual progress, and group progress.

The Microhost is one of the most well-established ILS in existence, having over fifteen years of experience and more installations than all other ILSs together. Studies on the use of Microhost have demonstrated impressive effectiveness in increasing academic achievement scores (Electronic Learning, 1986). However, the implementation of Microhost is relatively expensive and takes a strong commitment of resources, both financial and human.

Wicat System 300. The Wicat System 300 (Wicat Systems, 1984) employs a centrally located minicomputer that will support up to thirty work stations. Schools or agencies can also use IBM PC or Apple IIe microcomputers in place of the System 300 keyboards, although if they do, a microadapter linker must be purchased and installed. In 1986 there were approximately 150 Wicat systems in use across the United States.

Instructional software for the Wicat system is aimed at the basic skills for kindergarten through grade twelve, including reading, writing, language arts, mathematics, and related topics. Users of the system select the instructional topic from these areas. In the past, Wicat has worked cooperatively with the Plato computer-based instructional software developers to make the Plato series of courseware available with the Wicat system.

Houghton Mifflin's Dolphin System. The Dolphin System published by Houghton Mifflin (1985) uses Digital Equipment's microcomputer and is designed to be used in a laboratory. The instructional management component of the system tracks individual student progress, diagnoses weak areas, and prescribes appropriate coursework. There are approximately 75 school districts across the country using the Dolphin ILS System and instructional programs. The Dolphin software includes reading, language arts, and mathematics. The courseware addresses over 1,400 different skills and has been developed for elementary education through adult education.

The ICON System. The ICON is a Canadian-produced computer distributed by the Unisys Corporation (1987a). It represents one of the few microcomputer network systems designed specifically for education. The ICON System can include up to thirty-two work stations linked together throughout a school building. The system uses a Unix operating system and also has a PC-DOS emulator—allowing the use of most IBM PC software. ICON has a built in track ball that operates like a MacIntosh or IBM-PC mouse, as an alternative to keyboard entry. Speech output is also built into the system. Although the instructional software available is fairly extensive, the instructional management system can only be used with the remedial reading tutorial software published by Unisys.

The system's instructional software has been been developed under the auspices of the Ontario Ministry of Education and cuts across curricula and grade levels, from preschool through high school. Curriculum areas include reading, mathematics, science, and other topics. In addition to the software available through Unisys, public domain software that will run on the system is also available.

Generic Instructional Management Systems

As indicated earlier *generic instructional management systems* refer to those systems that provide instructional management and can be customized to support any instructional curriculum. These systems do not provide direct instruction on the computer; this is the main difference between generic instructional management systems and integrated learning systems. The term *generic* refers to the systems' ability to be customized to interact with locally developed curricula. A school system or university department can also use a generic instructional management system in association with a commercial textbook series adopted by the school system, or a specific textbook used by a professor.

Louisiana State Department of Education. At the end of 1986, *Electronic Learning Magazine,* a popular magazine aimed at educators interested in the use of computers, named John Guilbeau of Louisiana as Educator of the Year (Reinhold, 1986). Guilbeau is on the staff of the Louisiana State Department of Education. Over several years, he established two computer-managed instruction systems and helped train teachers and administrators to use them. In 1977, a special school district (SSD1) was set up in Louisiana to monitor the state-operated mental health, retardation, and correctional facilities. This state-wide school district serves about 1,700 students.

In 1981, SD1 administrators decided that in order to manage the new district better, they needed a computerized management information system. They asked Guilbeau to plan and implement it. Specifically, a system was needed to manage administrative and academic data on each student for each school so that each school's staff could develop certain reports, including individualized educational plans (IEPs). It was important that the system also provide data on each school for the central office so that it could maintain backup student files and school summary information for planning, managing, and reporting purposes. Guilbeau found what he was looking for in a system developed and sold by Education Turnkey Systems of Falls Church, Virginia. "Education Turnkey put a great deal of effort into modifying it for the district's specific needs," says Guilbeau, adding, "they gave us a Cadillac program" (Reinhold, 1986). The entire system cost around $150,000 or about $95 per student.

The Modularized Student Management System (MSMS), developed and sold by Education Turnkey, is programmed to run on IBM PC or the Apple IIe. Running the program requires two floppy disk drives with a card printer. The MSMS program can manage from 20 to 1,000 students, using floppy disks. It can also operate with a hard disk drive storage.

The MSMS emphasizes the management of administrative information about students. The instructional management capabilities are limited to the selection and printing of annual goals and objectives for individual students. Individual student files allow the storage of demographic data, testing data, and information about the program the student has received (i.e., courses, special classes, and special services). Installation of the MSMS requires technical expertise and consultation. With one day of training, however, personnel using the system find it easy to use.

The Hopkins Public Schools and The Mastery Management System. The Hopkins Public Schools, a school district in suburban Minneapolis, Minnesota for kindergarten through grade twelve has been involved for over ten years in the development and use of computer-based instructional management. The district has approximately 7,000 students and has developed instructional objectives for language arts, mathematics, science, and social studies for grades two through twelve. The CMI software program, named Mastery Management System, was developed by the staff of the district's Evaluation Center. The school system uses the program to score paper-and-pencil multiple-choice tests, using an optical mark card reader connected to the computer. The teacher turns the answer sheets over to an aide or school secretary, who feeds them into the computer and hands the results back to the teacher within an hour. The program gives teachers almost instant information on what students are and are not learning. With this information, the teachers help students achieve mastery of specific instructional objectives, improving the teachers' effectiveness.

The Hopkins Evaluation Center staff members indicate that the program is very popular and has been adopted by over 500 schools in forty-nine states (Sension, 1985). Houghton Mifflin now publishes the program, renamed The Houghton Mifflin Management System, which operates on an Apple IIe microcomputer, with a minimum of 64K memory. Two disk drives and a printer are required to operate the program. The program consists of a minimum of three disks with an optional study-help disk. Although an optical card/page reader is optional, most users take advantage of this feature. Without an optical mark reader, results of student testing must be entered at the keyboard, a much slower process.

A main feature of the program is the capability to allow the user to enter his or her own instructional objectives and resource information. System capacities include up to 400 instructional objectives— instructional resource information, 250 test keys (up to fifty questions per test), 900 students, twenty student/teacher groups, and 200 students per group. Fourteen reports (i.e., student status reports) and lists (i.e., student lists) can be generated by the program (Askeland, 1985). Figure 4.5 presents a chart showing the Mastery Management Systems organization, menus, and submenus.

The Jordan School District and The GEMS Program. The Jordan School District, in Salt Lake City, Utah, implemented a CMI program as early as 1976. At that time microcomputers with today's capabilities were not available. The school used a mainframe, or large central computer, to assist with the program. The goal-based educational management system (GEMS) was described by the district as "a computer supported manage-

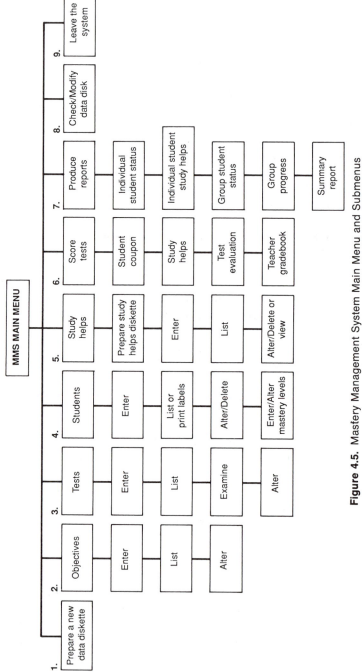

Figure 4.5. Mastery Management System Main Menu and Submenus

ment system developed to support diagnostic-prescriptive teaching for mastery learning.'' The district described the GEMS program as follows:

> Administrators, teachers, students, and parents were involved in determining the ''scope and sequence'' of the Reading Curriculum. This scope and sequence was divided into a series of goal units that spelled out the skills to be mastered at each grade level. The goal units were further organized into strands. For example, GEMS Reading was divided into 200 goal units to be covered from kindergarten through high school across six separate strands—phonics, structure, vocabulary, comprehension, study skills, and affective reading. Each goal unit was given an organizing number that identified the curriculum area, the grade level, the strand, and the goal unit number within the strand at that level. All information and material relating to a goal unit were coded by the goal unit number. Pre- and post-tests were provided for each goal, and placement tests for each strand were provided to help teachers identify the appropriate instructional level for each student. Multiple strategies and materials to aid in teaching for mastery were identified and coded to the GEMS Reading system. (Hofmeister, 1984, p. 5–6)

In the Jordan School District CMI program, each student in the system was first assessed in a goal area. This ''placement testing'' determined which specific objectives or units within a goal area had been mastered and which ones had not. The computer scored the placement test and provided suggestions to the teacher as to what learning strategies and materials would be appropriate (prescriptions). The computer report was, in effect, an individual study program for each pupil. By analyzing the progress of students through the specific curriculum units, staffs at the school and district levels were able to identify areas of weakness in the curriculum. The information was used to remediate these weaknesses. Alternative teaching strategies were developed, curriculum sequences were revised, instructional materials were changed, and in-service training programs were developed. The effect of these changes was then monitored by using the computer to analyze the achievement gains of pupils. Ineffective practices and materials were replaced.

This application of a CMI system resulted in a continuous process of intervention, evaluation, and program revision. In the Jordan School District, the effect of this process was substantial. Within a two-year period the average reading comprehension score jumped ten percentile points, from 45 to 55, and the average vocabulary score jumped twenty-one percentile points, from 45 to 66. The CMI program in the Jordan School District was able to demonstrate impressive accomplishments. An extensive two-year validation study (over 15,000 students) on the reading program supported by the management system demonstrated significant gains in favor of the GEMS instruction-supported students. The use of card readers to score and prescribe from the criterion referenced test considerably reduced cost factors, increased access, and reduced time delays. The GEMS program has been replicated in a number of other districts and states (Hofmeister, 1984).

The Unisys MicroCASTs Computer-Managed Instruction System. The MicroCASTS CMI System (Unisys Corporation, 1987b) is one of the most powerful and comprehensive generic instructional management systems available. The program can be installed on an individual Unisys microcomputer with 10 to 30 megabytes of hard disk capacity, or it can be installed on a hard disk server station with up to thirty-two stations. A prototype CMI program was developed by the University of North Carolina at Chapel Hill, under contract with the University Sponsored Research Office of Unisys Corporation (1987b). Based on the prototype, Unisys revised and expanded the CMI program into the final system released in 1987.

The MicroCASTS CMI system has been used with success in a number of school systems. In Chapel Hill, North Carolina, the system was used in coordination with the Scott-Foresman basal reading series at the elementary school level. In Illinois, the system was used in a secondary school to manage instructional information for social studies.

Figure 4.6 displays the menu flowchart for the MicroCAST Instructional Management System. The system has several utility features that are frequently missing from other CMI programs. The group definition functions allow the creation of different user groups. For example, in an installation in a university, each department might represent a user group. Once established, instructional management for a large number of subjects or courses for that group can be implemented. Password definition is also a unique and important component. Each user must have a password established to access the program. Password definitions can be designed so that users can access student and curriculum information in the CMI system related only to their instructional responsibilities. Viewing information related to other grades, teachers, and/or groups can be made impossible. The password feature generates security and privacy.

Another feature of the MicroCASTs CMI system is the capability to configure the program to read any optical scan form. A subprogram allows the user to establish the parameters for the type of optical scanner and the specific scan form being used. Although this type of interface with the user takes more time to learn, once learned it provides a much more powerful and flexible system.

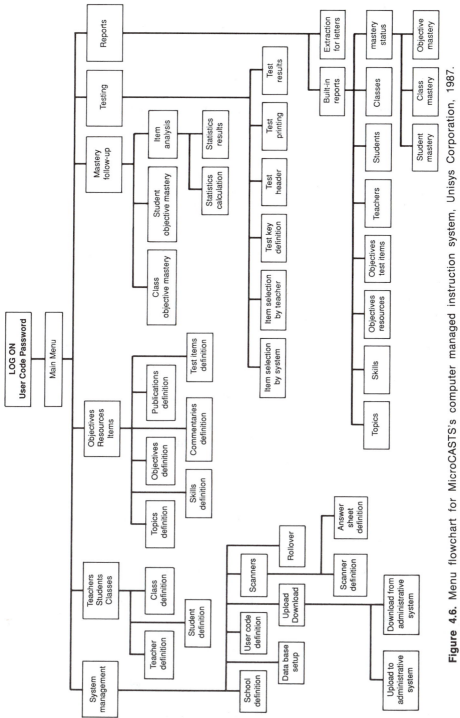

Figure 4.6. Menu flowchart for MicroCASTS's computer managed instruction system, Unisys Corporation, 1987. Reprinted with permision of Unisys Corporation.

Capacities of the CMI program, such as number of subjects, number of students, number of instructional objectives, and so on, are limited only by the configuration of the hardware involved. Printouts include the standard reports and lists: individual objective mastery, correlated resources and materials, group objective mastery, group progress summaries, objectives, test questions, test results, teachers list, students list, subjects list, and prescriptions.

The South Carolina Department of Youth Services and the IMS Program. The South Carolina Department of Youth Services has successfully implemented the use of a CMI system to meet the instructional management needs required in the State of South Carolina. The Department of Youth Services operates a twelve-month comprehensive education program for youthful offenders. The school program is directed by the South Carolina Department of Education as a special school district. When a student first enters the program, he or she is sent to the Reception and Evaluation Center for several days, during which time a comprehensive evaluation is conducted to assess the student's educational needs. As a result of the evaluation, an individual educational plan is developed, and the student is placed in one of several avaliable secondary schools. Approximately twenty new students are evaluated each week.

To assist with the development of an instructional plan, the Instructional Management System developed by Lillie and Edwards (1986a) was adopted for use and customized, using the curriculum scope and sequence and instructional objectives established in 1985 for the South Carolina Basic Skills Assessment Program. Curriculum and instructional objectives were established for the basic skills areas of reading, mathematics, and writing.

To measure individual mastery status and progress, the California Achievement Tests (CAT) are used across grades on a regularly scheduled basis. At the Department of Youth Services, the CAT is routinely administered to each entering student during the evaluation process. The resulting CAT scores are entered into a microcomputer with the use of an optical scanner and the IMS software program. The IMS program (1) scores the results of the CAT, (2) interprets instructional objective mastery based on criterion established by the department, (3) establishes a series of instructional objectives projected (to be worked on) for the student, and (4) suggests instructional materials and/or activities for working toward mastery of each projected objective. The individual objective mastery report illustrated earlier in Figure 4.4 is printed and used as an instructional plan for each student evaluated. The plan follows the student to one of the Department of Youth Services schools and/or to a public school, depending on the student's placement.

During the 1985–1986 school year, the Instructional Management System was used in a federally supported microcomputer project in the Durham County, North Carolina Public Schools (1986) to track progress of students with learning disabilities and emotional handicaps. The individual objective mastery reports generated by the IMS were used as a component of the individualized education program required by the federal government and the states. Information about objectives mastered and objectives projected (to be worked on) proved very helpful in coordinating individual students' instructional programs between the special teachers and the regular or mainstream teachers.

The Main Menu, as illustrated in Figure 4.7, is the most frequently used menu in the IMS program.

As is typical of many of the CMI programs, there are several functions that can be selected from the Main Menu. The Print Reports option prints reports. The Testing Menu establishes test keys, administers tests on the computer, scans results of tests with an optical scanner, prints tests, and/or allows the user to enter the results of tests into the program. Update/Review Student Information allows entering, editing, or deleting information on a student. New students are added to the list through this function before other functions of the program are used. As discussed previously, the Update/Review IMS setup is the function used initially to set up a data disk with a curriculum scope and sequence, instructional objectives, test questions, and prescriptions (or reference materials).

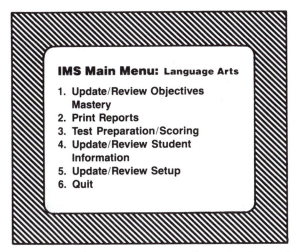

Figure 4.7. The main menu screen from the Instructional Management System

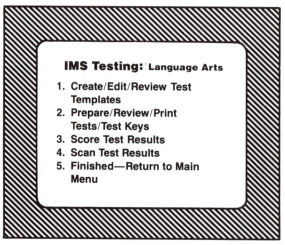

Figure 4.8. The IMS testing menu screen

Figure 4.8 illustrates the IMS Testing Menu. This menu is typical of CMI testing menus.

Subject-Specific Instructional Management Systems

A number of the leading textbook publishers have developed instructional management software that is correlated with their basal textbook series in language arts. The major emphases of these programs are on test scoring, test analysis, individual progress files maintenance, and reports that summarize each student's progress. Six of the leading textbook publishers are marketing instructional management systems correlated to their basal reading series. These are Ginn; Harcourt Brace Jovanovich; Scott–Foresman; Houghton Mifflin; Macmillan; and Holt, Rinehart and Winston. Three of these are discussed briefly.

Class II Reading Testbank. Class II, a data management program published by Holt, Rinehart and Winston (1984), is correlated to the publisher's reading series. They also have versions to accompany their English, science, mathematics, and social studies textbooks. Different versions of the Class II program operate on the Apple II microcomputer series or IBM PC compatible microcomputers. The program provides test administration, test scoring and analysis, item analysis, and objective mastery progress reports. Three disks are required to run the program: a program disk, a student disk, and a curriculum disk. The student disk can contain mastery information for up to forty students. The curriculum disk allows the teacher or instructor to enter, edit, or display up to 500 objectives. The Class II program can also be used as a generic instructional management, allowing users to enter their own objectives. Class II offers the basic features found in most instructional management systems. Users will need introductory training to use it comfortably.

SERIES r Instructional Management System. SERIES r, Instructional Management System published by Macmillan Company (1985), is similar to Class II but it does not allow the user to make changes in the setup. It is designed to be used with the Macmillan SERIES r Reading Program. The program will score tests provided by the publisher, store individual achievement data, generate prescriptions based on test results, and print test results and student progress. The program requires a main program disk and student record disks. Multiple student record disks can be maintained with one program disk. The SERIES r software is available only for the Apple II series of microcomputers.

SELECTING AND IMPLEMENTING
A COMPUTER-BASED INSTRUCTIONAL
MANAGEMENT SYSTEM

As we documented earlier in this chapter, mastery learning instructional methods and procedures have proven very effective in increasing academic achievement of students. The mastery learning research suggests that schools can provide not only equality of educational opportunity but also equality of educational results (Bloom, 1976). Mastery learning supported by computer technology innovations appears to fit well with the educational trends in the 1980s—accountability, academic achievement, educational opportunity equality, and the infusion of modern electronic technology in the schools. Why then isn't mastery learning, supported by computer technology, more widely received and used in the delivery of instruction? Unfortunately, there is no clear or simple answer to this question.

Clearly, widespread use of computer-based instructional management systems for instructional purposes will occur only with the acceptance and application of mastery learning theory. At least part of the reason for the slow growth of the use of mastery learning techniques has been the lack of emphasis in teacher training methods courses. Many teachers and education administrators are unaware of the research support for mastery learning and are not knowledgeable about mastery learning techniques.

Unfortunately, so far the main motivation leading to decisions to implement CMI systems does not seem to involve the goal of improving instruction. Many educational leaders are more motivated to implement CMI systems to gather data on the general effectiveness of their schools than to provide information for instructional planning. Their main reasons for implementing CMI systems involve the need for evaluation data to meet accountablity demands.

Based on the assumption that many educators are more interested in improving their methods of instruction than in evaluating their effectiveness, the following discussion will focus on issues that should be addressed as schools plan for the implementation of computer-based instructional management systems.

Staff Attitudes and Training

Most educators, particularly public school teachers, are well acquainted with educational innovations. They have been involved with innovations mandated either at the state level or the local education administrative level. As a result of a flurry of special studies, commission reports, and council reports (e.g., Carnegie Foundation, 1984), new programs have been mandated with names like Basic Education Program, Career Ladder Program, Teacher Evaluation System, and Effective Schools Program. Classroom teachers have had little involvement in the planning of the new programs but are expected to incorporate them into their already extremely busy work schedules. Consequently, new curriculum theories such as mastery learning are likely to be received with some skepticism by the staff members who have the most to gain, the classroom instructors. If mastery learning techniques supported by computer technology are to be successful, however, it is essential that administrators and teachers enthusiastically accept mastery learning theory and instructional strategies. Installing a computer system with good CMI software will be of little value in an instructional environment without dedicated, motivated, and energetic teachers.

Organizational Issues

A CMI system can be implemented in an educational setting at a number of different levels, from an individual instructor application to an agency-wide level. Although mastery learning theory and techniques may not be part of a total faculty or school system instructional philosophy, individual teachers or instructors may follow mastery learning principles very closely. When a single instructor is adopting a CMI system, microcomputer systems with low storage capacity on floppy disks may be adequate. Usually the cost of microcomputers without a hard disk drive is relatively low, and the CMI is uncomplicated and easy to use. On the negative side, microcomputers using floppy disk drives exclusively operate relatively slowly compared to microcomputers with hard disk drives and/or mini-computers, and the flexibility or availability of options is limited. Realistically, only a few teachers will have an instructional materials budget that will allow them to purchase a lower-cost CMI system to use with an already available floppy drive microcomputer.

Because of the initial costs involved in purchasing software and the additional hardware needed, such as an optical scanner and printer, it is more feasible for educational agencies to implement a CMI system within a total unit of the organization. This unit may be an elementary school building, a department within a university, or a department within a public school such as Special Education. When installing a building-wide system, consideration must be given to establishing a school-wide curricular scope and sequence. In this manner, the unit would be mandating the use of the same sequence of subjects, subskills, instructional objectives, test questions, and instructional resources or prescriptions for all instructors and across levels of instruction. At a school-wide or department-wide level, more students, tests, objectives, and so forth will no doubt be needed. Accordingly, a CMI system with larger capacities of storage will be necessary.

If a decision is made to implement a CMI system across the total school system, additional issues must be considered. A computer system that will allow communication across several computers, or computer terminals placed in various buildings, will be desirable. With a large installation, more hard disk capacity will be needed to run the system efficiently. One of the most important aspects of a large CMI installation, either at a building level or system-wide level, is the need for dedicated leadership and coordination. It is a big mistake to install and implement a CMI program without providing release time to a staff member for coordination of the effort. The use of a CMI system at any level takes training and experience. Busy classroom teachers will not have the time to take on the additional responsibilities of managing the system. The use of a CMI system by teachers already using a mastery learning approach to instruction will save teachers time only if there is an appointed coordinator who has some time set aside for coordinating the use of the system.

Technology Issues

A rule of thumb in considering the use of a CMI system is that the more powerful and flexible the system, the more complex and difficult it will be to use. Educators primarily use relatively easy-to-use hardware and software—turn the machine on and follow the directions. With hardware systems and software programs that provide the user with many different features within a particular application, use of the system becomes more difficult to learn. The need for easy-to-use computer systems across a variety of applications is somewhat unique to education. In business and commercial applications, most computer systems are installed for one or two primary applications. In these situations, the software is installed as part of the hardware purchase and configuration. The technical experts who market the application do not leave the user until training has taken place and the application is running smoothly. A few staff members become experts at running the system, and the technical expert from the computer company remains on call for any trouble-shooting that is necessary.

In education, multiple applications are expected to run on the same microcomputer with a minimum of difficulty—tutorials, word processing, file programs, spreadsheets, games, and so on. When it is important to have a microcomputer system on which a user can easily run a variety of application software programs, the flexibility and power of each of the applications will be sacrificed. Perhaps one of the reaons that CMI software systems have not met with widespread use in education is that users have tried to run these large and complicated software programs on microcomputers that are not designed for that type of task. Also, when the computer is to be shared with a number of other users and applications, small reconfigurations needed for one application (such as resetting dip switches on a printer or on a communication card installed in the microcomputer) will cause problems with other applications.

As described, there are a number of issues to consider in planning the installation of a CMI system. Positive attitudes toward the use of mastery learning and computer technology can be developed through involvement of the instructional staff in the planning as well as through adequate training. The size of the instructional unit that will be using the system must be considered, along with the type and power of the computer that will be used to run the CMI system. Perhaps most important, a staff member should be given an adequate amount of time within his or her job responsibilities to coordinate the use of the CMI system.

SUMMARY

Computer-based instructional management is potentially one of the most promising applications of computer technology to the instructional process. The data and information management capabilities provided by computers provide teachers with a quick and easy way to organize and retrieve instructionally related information on individual students and/or various groupings of students. Effective instruction cannot be maintained for any meaningful length of time without effective instructional information management. The relationship between mastery learning practices and the use of instructional management systems is extremely clear. To be effective, instruction must include conveying instructional expectations through the use of objectives, frequent monitoring and testing, planning instructional activities based on objective mastery, and precise and frequent feedback on performance to students.

Most computer-based management systems allow the school system the option of using their own curricular scope and sequence. That is, the local school system's curriculum, organized by subject, subskills, instructional objectives, mastery test questions, and instruction prescriptions (or activities), can be typed into the instructional management software system. This capability separates CMI and/or IMS systems from integrated learning systems that provide excellent instructional management but lock in the curriculum—usually to correlate with commercially available materials and testing materials.

Computer-based management systems provide a comprehensive array of components that are designed to support effective instruction. These components include the capability to (1) enter and/or edit the curriculum content; (2) enter and file information on individual students; (3) administer and/or score and analyze individual students' tests; and (4) update individual student mastery files, providing an array of different reports indicating individual and/or group instructional progress. With the increasing attention to accountability and basic skills training, computer-based instructional management will play a larger and larger role in American education.

PUTTING THE BOOK TO WORK

Read through the following questions, and then review the source pages indicated. Responding to these questions, either in your mind or on paper, will provide you with a comprehensive review of the material presented in this chapter.

Question	*Source*
1. Why is computer-managed instruction presented as a component of the instructional process, as opposed to a component of educational administration?	54
2. How do integrated learning systems differ from generic CMI systems?	54–55
3. How does CMI facilitate a mastery learning approach to instruction?	56–58

4. Which effective teaching principles are facilitated through the use of CMI systems?   56–59

5. What does a CMI curriculum setup consist of?   60

6. What are the four components of a comprehensive CMI system?   60–66

7. What instructional and instruction-related activities is a pupil engaged in when interacting with an integrated learning system?   68–75

8. Which of the three types of CMI systems is the most limited in scope?   84–85

9. Why do CMI systems seem to be more popular in agencies that have mandated basic skills programs?   54–58

CHAPTER 5

Assessment and Evaluation

Objectives

When you have finished reading this chapter, you should be able to do the following:

1. Cite two reasons why computer-based testing can improve a classroom teacher's instructional effectiveness.
2. Compare and contrast four categories of testing and measurement activities that take place in the schools.
3. Cite the seven main components of comprehensive computer-based testing programs.
4. Describe a "test item bank" and explain how it is used.
5. Cite and describe two computer-based methods of administering a test to a student.
6. Define *test key* and describe how it is used in computer-based test scoring.
7. Identify the major role and function of testing in a typical classroom.
8. Describe how computer-based testing programs are able to produce instructional plans.
9. Define and describe expert systems, artificial intelligence, and computer-based error analysis.

INTRODUCTION: TESTING
IN TODAY'S SCHOOLS

If there is any one aspect of the public school curriculum that has been a focus of the school reform movement in the last five to ten years, it is assessment and evaluation of student progress. Most of the fifty states in the United States have established some type of state-wide achievement testing program. As a result, most school systems in the country administer system-wide tests every year. Standardized achievement testing is big business in American education. To cut costs and increase efficiency, large testing companies, such as CBT/McGraw-Hill, Educational Testing Service, or Harcourt Brace, employ computer-assisted test scoring and analysis. Standardized achievement tests like the California Achievement Tests, the Stanford Achievement Tests, and the Iowa Basic Skills Tests are all scored with computers. The process involves pupils placing their response choice for each question on an optical mark scan form. The scan forms are sent to the publisher, and using an optical mark scanner, the publisher reads the test results into the computer. The computer scores the results, and in some cases conducts a short interpretation of the student's academic strengths and weaknesses. Through the years, computer scoring has proven reliable and very cost effective.

Assessment and testing activities at the individual classroom level are no less important. A significant amount of an individual teacher's time is devoted to assessment and evaluation activities. Most teachers, following effective instruction practices, evaluate the progress of their students at least twice each semester—at mid-semester and at the end of the semester. Many teachers assess progress more frequently than that. Student assessment is not a task that a teacher can undertake by setting aside an hour or two each semester. When Betty Coburn, a third-grade teacher at a local elementary school, decides to give her class of twenty-eight students a progress examination, she will have to perform a number of tasks. Although her teacher training experiences helped develop the professional skills needed to construct, administer, score, and interpret tests, she was not prepared for the amount of time these tasks would take. First, Betty Coburn has to construct the test. Through the years, she has developed and collected test items that measure the extent to which a student has mastered each of the instructional objectives that she has established for her third-grade language arts class. Occasionally, she has thrown out items that she felt did not measure an objective accurately and added new items. To prepare her test, she goes through her "bank" of test items and decides which items to use for this particular test. From a total of 250 items, ten items for each of twenty-five instructional objectives that she has established for language arts, she selects fifty items—five items for each of the ten instructional objectives she is measuring on this test.

After selecting the items, Betty Coburn must type the test. While her husband and two children are watching a special program that night on television, guess what she is doing? Right—she is typing her midterm examination! The next morning, before school begins, she uses the copy machine to make twenty-eight copies of the test. During the third period she administers the test to her third-grade class. The hard work is just beginning. Knowing that one of the effective teaching practices (on which she is evaluated twice a year) that separates good teachers from mediocre and poor teachers is prompt and frequent performance monitoring and feedback, Betty Coburn spends that evening scoring and grading the tests. The scoring process involves checking each answer on the student's test against the answer key. With twenty-eight students and fifty questions on the test, by the time she has finished, she has looked at 1,400 responses.

After totaling the raw scores for each student, again dealing with twenty-eight students and fifty questions, she converts each student's total raw score to a percentage score. Although she bases grades on an established criterion (90 percent and above earns an A), Betty Coburn is interested in obtaining the mean score and distribution of scores for the class. She will use this information to help her determine the effectiveness of instruction and plan for individual and group instruction for the next eight weeks.

Does Betty Coburn represent the typical teacher in the procedures and the amount of time devoted to testing and feedback to students? Yes, she does! As we discussed in chapter 2, good teachers test frequently and provide timely feedback on performance.

Although computer-based test scoring has been employed for a number of years by the large testing companies, the value for classroom teachers is just beginning to be recognized. Use of a computer can not only extensively reduce the clerical tasks involved in assessment and evaluation but also improve the quality of the test and the comprehensive nature of the feedback to students.

The purpose of this chapter is to acquaint you with the procedures and techniques involved in using the computer to assist with the tasks of constructing tests, administering tests, scoring tests, interpreting tests, monitoring student progress, and reporting that progress to students and parents.

To understand the use of computers in the testing process, it is first necessary to understand the basic purposes of testing in schools and the type of tests used for those purposes. The general purposes for testing and measurement activities in schools can be divided into four main categories: (1) screening, (2) diagnosis, (3) educational assessment, and (4) evaluation of instruction. Table 5.1 provides a brief description and comparison of these categories.

Computer-based testing can be applied more appropriately in some of these categories than in others. A brief review of the various uses of tests in schools will be presented here. For a comprehensive review of measurement activities in education, we suggest that you read one of the many educational evaluation and measurement texts available (e.g., Gay, 1985).

Tests can be divided into two main types: normative referenced tests and criterion referenced tests. When a school is involved in a testing activity for screening or diagnostic purposes, a student's performance on the test is compared to the performance of other students who have taken the same test. A test that provides comparative information is normative referenced and has been standardized. Test standardization involves giving the test, following a specific set of standard procedures, to a large, representative group of students. Using the results of the standardization testing, normative data are established for the test.

Criterion referenced tests are frequently used when the purpose of the testing is educational assessment and/or evaluation. A student's performance on a criterion referenced test is interpreted in relationship to the requirements of a specific set of tasks that the test has been designed to measure. For example, if the task is to decode consonant-vowel-consonant (C-V-C) words correctly, the student may be asked to read and pronounce the following words from a page: *dog, log, hog, dig, pig, big, cat, sat, bat,* and *rat.* If the criterion for demonstrating the ability to

TABLE 5.1. TESTS AND MEASUREMENT IN SCHOOLS

Category	Purpose	Type
Screening	A quick, economical procedure to determine which members of a large population (e.g., all kindergarten pupils in a school system) need further, in-depth diagnostic testing	N
Diagnosis	An in-depth educational and/or psychological study to find causes and to *classify* (e.g., learning disability, dyslexia, mental retardation)	N
Educational assessment	To determine the presence or absence of specific skills to provide information for *instructional planning*	C
Evaluation	To determine the current status of student(s) or program in relationship to achievement expectations and primarily used to assign *grades*	N/C

N = normative reference; C = criterion reference

decode consonant-vowel-consonant words is established as the correct recognition of 90 percent of the C-V-C words presented, the student must correctly identify nine out of the ten words. With criterion tests, a comparison as to how other students did on the test is not being made. Instead, decisions are based on whether or not the student met the criteria established for each item or set of items.

Decisions about which objectives in the curriculum have been mastered by a specific student can be made by using a criterion referenced test that has been developed specifically for that purpose. When a teacher is involved in testing for purposes of assessment and/or evaluation as described in Table 5.1, most testing activities will often involve the use of criterion referenced testing instruments. Today, however, standardized achievement testing for the purpose of student evaluation represents the largest application of computer-based testing activities. Testing companies and educators have found that the use of computers for scoring and reporting standardized test results significantly reduces labor and costs, and at the same time increases accuracy and efficiency. In a nationwide survey of 300 large school systems, conducted by the Unisys Technology Project at the University of North Carolina, Chapel Hill (1987), 79 percent of the school systems surveyed reported that they use computers to score, store, retrieve, and print test reports.

COMPONENTS OF COMPUTER-BASED TESTING SYSTEMS

There is a certain amount of overlap between the components of computer-based testing programs and computer-managed instruction systems, discussed in the previous chapter. All comprehensive CMI software programs contain testing components. However, not all testing software programs contain the information and data management components found in CMI systems. The main differences between these two types of software is that the test development programs do not address the management of test results as thoroughly as CMI systems do. On the other hand, testing systems often include features directly related to the testing that many CMI systems do not have. For example, most testing software programs include teacher-controlled grading processes to translate test results into grades for the students. In addition, most computer-based testing systems include a component that allows the instructor to conduct an analysis of the tests themselves—an item analysis procedure.

The seven main components of computer-based testing programs are (1) developing a test item bank, (2) test construction, (3) test administration, (4) test scoring, (5) interpretation and analysis of results, (6) item

TABLE 5.2. COMPONENTS OF COMPUTER-BASED TESTING PROGRAMS

Component	Computer Function
Test item bank development	Categorizes each item/question entered by skill and instructional objective and saves and files the item. Most test banks can file several hundred items.
Test construction	Organizes the items selected from the test bank into a specific test.
Test administration	Prints tests, presents test on computer, or allows use of optical scanner sheets for recording answers.
Test scoring	Allows creation of test keys, compares student responses to test key, and scores test.
Test interpretation	Allows creation of interpretation key that provides decision-making parameters. Compares test results with interpretation key and prints summary interpretation statements.
Item analysis	Saves test results across students and test items. Computes difficulty level (percent passing item) and discrimination index (percent of high-scoring and percent of low-scoring students passing items).
Results reporting	Stores and prints individual and group objective mastery reports and summaries.

analysis and test refinement, and (7) reporting test results. Table 5.2 presents these main components and the function of the computer for each of them.

Constructing Item Banks and Tests

Computer-based testing incorporates two of the main analysis capabilities that computers provide: (1) information management and (2) conditional responding. Using a computer to construct a test is a specific application of the information management capabilities of the computer. Entering and/or editing test items is a word-processing application. Selecting test items from a pool of items to construct a specific test uses the relational information data base capabilities of the computer. That is, the computer "remembers" where a particular test item is stored, usually through the use of a code, and can retrieve that item to place it in a test that is being constructed.

Like Betty Coburn, most teachers spend a lot of time during their careers constructing and preparing tests. Most computer-based testing software programs available facilitate the test construction process by establishing a test item bank. An item bank is a systematically organized collection of test items, from which specific items can be selected to construct a test. Most definitions of item banks are very general in nature.

Millman and Arter (1984) define item banks as simply "a relatively large collection of easily accessible test questions." Different terms frequently used to test item banks include *item pools, item banks, question banks,* and *item collections* (Millman & Arter, 1984). In most computer testing programs, test item banks are organized so that items are indexed by the specific skill or instructional objective that the items measure. In this respect, the item bank is domain referenced or criterion referenced.

Ideally, each item in a test bank will be a valid and reliable measure of the skill it is designed to measure. Some educators attach a difficulty level to each of the test items contained in an item bank. Others argue, however, that the item either measures a specific skill or it doesn't—and the difficulty level is expressed by the skill or instructional objective itself and not by the test item.

The advantages of using item banks for the preparation of tests are quite obvious. Teacher time devoted to test preparation can be reduced. Tests and test items do not have to be rewritten each time a test is to be given because alternate versions of the same test can be easily developed. This is sometimes necessary to prevent rote learning of specific questions and/or responses.

Using an item bank requires that the teacher be fairly well organized. A certain amount of structure is necessary in the curricular scope and sequence, such as the use of specific sequences of instructional objectives. This will improve the overall quality of the teaching because the process of selecting or constructing a classification system for the items will help clarify the instructional goals and objectives. Usually, a particular computer-based testing program will be used by a number of teachers in the same building or school system. This shared system approach may lead to a controlled process of reviewing and adding items to the test bank, resulting in the selection of higher-quality items to place in the test bank.

All computer-based test item banks have the same basic components. After the user selects a subprogram for entering test items (or questions) from a main menu, he or she will be provided with a routine to correlate the items to enter into the bank, with a skill area and a specific objective in that skill area. After the skill and objective correlation is indicated, the user will type in one or more questions to be saved in the test bank. For example, Screen A and B in Figure 5.1 illustrate one approach used to identify the correlated skill and instructional objective as test items are typed into the program. In Screen A, the user selects the skill area that will move him or her to Screen B. In this illustration, skill area 1, Word Identification, was selected. At the top of Screen B, the skill area selected from Screen A is indicated: "Skill . . . Language Arts—Word Ident." As can be seen on this screen, the user has indicated that five test items

Screen A

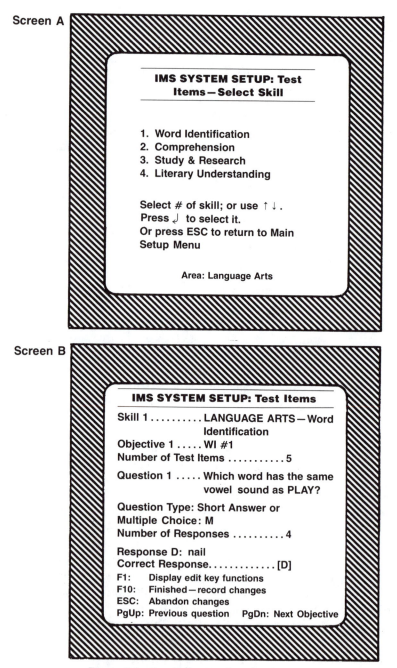

IMS SYSTEM SETUP: Test Items — Select Skill

1. Word Identification
2. Comprehension
3. Study & Research
4. Literary Understanding

Select # of skill; or use ↑↓.
Press ↵ to select it.
Or press ESC to return to Main
Setup Menu

Area: Language Arts

Screen B

IMS SYSTEM SETUP: Test Items

Skill 1 . . . . LANGUAGE ARTS — Word
                        Identification
Objective 1 . . . . . WI #1
Number of Test Items 5

Question 1 . . . . . Which word has the same
                        vowel sound as PLAY?

Question Type: Short Answer or
Multiple Choice: M
Number of Responses 4

Response D: nail
Correct Response. . . . . [D]
F1:   Display edit key functions
F10:   Finished — record changes
ESC: Abandon changes
PgUp: Previous question   PgDn: Next Objective

Figure 5.1. Creating a test item bank

will be created for Objective WI.1. The questions are typed into the program, using a word-editing process. On Screen B, question 1 has already been typed: "Which word has the same vowel sound as PLAY?" To enter the four alternative responses to this question, the program prompts the user to type in Response A. After Response A is entered, the program prompts the user to enter Response B. In this example there are four responses. Response D (or 4) is *nail,* which is the correct answer.

Although all four responses cannot be seen here, Screen B illustrates a completed question, with Response D indicated as the correct response.

Most testing programs allow zero to five possible responses. It is assumed that if no responses are indicated, the question is an open-ended, short-answer essay question that can be printed as part of a test but cannot be scored by the system. With a multiple-choice question, usually up to five different responses can be entered. After the responses are each entered, the program will ask the user to indicate the correct response. Different testing software programs have different routines for entering test items into the item bank. Most of them, however, share these basic instructions.

1. Identify the skill area and instructional objectives associated with the item(s) to be entered.
2. Type in the item.
3. Type in the responses, if appropriate.
4. Indicate the correct response, if appropriate.

The capacity of the item bank is an important consideration that varies widely across the various programs available. Some programs are limited in capacity because they are designed to run on microcomputers, such as an Apple IIe, that are readily available to teachers. Before a decision is made about what software program is to be used for constructing tests, it is wise to respond to the following questions.

1. How many different skill areas will you have in the system?
2. How many instructional objectives will you have in each of the skill areas?
3. How many questions do you intend to have "on file" in the bank, correlated with each instructional objective?
4. What is the maximum number of items you will need on any one test?
5. Do you want the capability to select items or do you want the program randomly to select the items for you?

Based on your responses to these questions and other considerations (such as the ease of use and the cost of the software), you should review the programs available to select the one that best addresses your needs.

Constructing a Test

Once the questions are on file in the item bank, specific tests can be constructed. Different software programs use different procedures for constructing a test. One approach used by some testing software programs is to select the items to be included by an item code number. Using this process, the teacher peruses the items measuring a particular skill and/or objective and makes a note of the code of each item he or she wants to include on the test. The code numbers are then entered into the program on a screen designed for that purpose. Another approach is the development of a test key for each test that is constructed. This process requires the teacher to name the test, the test item number, the test item from the item bank, and the correct response for the item. This process is repeated until all the items to be included on the test have been selected. With this procedure, multiple test keys can be developed and electronically filed to be used at any time. When a specific test is to be given, the teacher needs only to indicate which test. The program will retrieve that test key, construct the test, and if desired, print a copy of it.

Test Administration

Once a test has been constructed, there are several options for administering it. The most common procedure for administering a test is simply to give each student a copy. Each student will indicate his or her response for each question by marking or circling one of the possible answers for each question. This approach to administering a test leaves quite a lot of time-consuming work—entering each student's response to each question into the computer by the keyboard.

A test administration option that is becoming more and more popular is the use of an optical scanner. An optical scanner is a piece of equipment that can be connected to a computer via a cable to read electronically information from an optical scan sheet or card. Using a lead pencil, students indicate their responses to each question by making a dark mark in a designated spot. When the card is sent through the scanner, the light-sensitive device "reads" the student's responses and sends information to the computer indicating which responses were marked. The computer program checks a specific student's responses with the test key, which indicates the correct response for each question. The computer-assisted test-scoring program then scores the student's test and saves that student's test results.

Almost all the large testing companies use optical scanners for scoring their standardized achievement tests. Even with the use of scanners, it is frequently several weeks before a local school system receives the results of school-wide testing from the commercial testing company. This delay is primarily caused by the large numbers of tests these companies are handling on a daily basis. More and more school personnel are beginning to use optical scanners for test scoring at the local level. There are at least two major advantages for conducting a scanning operation locally. First, the time for receiving test results can be cut from six weeks to six days. With a faster feedback process, test results can be used for instructional planning for individuals and for groups. The second major benefit is the cost savings. With the cost of computers, optical scanners, and test-scoring software decreasing each year, a school system can realize a substantial savings by conducting its optical scanning and test scoring locally.

On the other hand, there are some serious hazards to avoid when using optical scanners. When students have to translate their response choices onto an optical scan sheet or card, the potential for a translation error is increased. A student may not mark the box that she or he intended to mark. When using an optical scan sheet for scoring, students must not only come up with the right answer but also be sure they marked the right box on the scan sheet. This introduces an additional step and an additional possibility of error. As a result, the reliability of the testing process may suffer. This may be particularly true with younger students, still working on eye-hand coordination and organization skills.

Another problem frequently encountered when using optical scanners is within the scanner itself. Optical scanners can be temperamental. Usually the information on a scan card is read appropriately, but occasionally a problem may occur. As has been the case with many developing technologies, optical scanners can sometimes be unreliable. If a pencil mark is not heavy enough on a scan sheet, it may not be read correctly. Other problems may arise in relationship to the position of the mark on a card. The optical scanner is quite sensitive and occasionally may need to be adjusted. Usually this means a frantic call to a technician employed by the company that manufactures and/or sells the optical scanner. Invariably, there will be problems in the middle of scoring several hundred scan sheets, with a number of teachers anxiously waiting for the return of their test results. Even with these problems, however, optical scanners used in tandem with test-scoring software programs are here to stay. Although they are not without their special set of problems, they can improve the timely use of test results in supporting the effective instruction principles and practices discussed in chapter 2.

On-Line Testing

The use of an optical scanner can be bypassed by having students take tests on a computer. Taking a test directly on a computer is frequently referred to as *on-line* testing. On-line testing presents several advantages, but not without raising a few issues. The most obvious advantage of computer testing is the reduction of time the instructor devotes to the administration and scoring of tests. Tests do not have to be handed out and collected, and the scores are immediately available. With a class of thirty students, individually scoring each student's test takes time, particularly with relatively long tests. In addition to the time considerations, the test administration procedures become more uniform, and there is less chance for students to be given different directions; the computer will give the same directions to each student. The elimination of scoring errors, the possibility of which is increased with the use of optical scanners, is another advantage of on-line testing. If the correct answer for each question is accurately recorded in the computer test key, the computer will not make a clerical mistake.

Although the advantages to on-line testing, particularly the time-saving argument, are attractive, there are a number of unresolved issues. First, does taking a test on the computer change the nature of the task being measured? If a student took the same or alternate, equal form of a test on a computer and in paper-and-pencil format, would he or she perform equally well in both situations? The few studies conducted to investigate this question have demonstrated a high level of reliability between the two modes of taking the same criterion referenced test (Hasselbring & Crossland, 1982). However, more investigations need to be conducted before it is assumed that the medium itself does not alter the performance. At this point, it is quite clear that the administration of standardized tests on a computer is inappropriate unless the normative data established for the test were developed through on-line testing. Presenting a standardized test that has been developed through paper-and-pencil established norms by means of a computer is inappropriate.

On-line testing also raises questions of a more technical nature. It is assumed that each student has equal skill in using a computer keyboard for responding to test questions. This may not be the case, and may consequently be a source of bias and error. A student who knows the correct response but has difficulty using the keyboard (finding keys) may make mistakes for reasons other than not knowing the content called for on the test.

With a paper-and-pencil test, a student may be using a strategy of answering all the questions that he or she clearly knows and skipping more difficult questions. When all the items are reviewed, the student then goes back and takes more time on the items that were skipped. On-line testing programs should allow the student the same test-taking strategy choices as does paper-and-pencil testing, without introducing difficult-to-follow procedures. With some of the on-line testing programs available, skipping items, reviewing items, or changing responses is either impossible or quite difficult. Figure 5.2 presents an example of on-line screens.

Aside from these issues, there is the question of the availability of the number of computer stations needed to accommodate on-line testing. Even though today many schools have established a computer laboratory with multiple microcomputers and/or computer terminals, rarely are

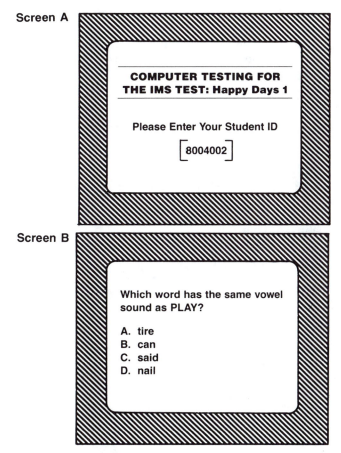

Figure 5.2. Typical screens from an on-line testing program

there enough computer stations available for each student in the class. Therefore, schedules will have to be arranged to allow smaller groups of students to take a test together at one sitting. If there is only one computer available to a teacher or classroom, on-line testing can only be accommodated through a sequential testing schedule.

Although there is increasing interest in and consideration of on-line testing, most of the current activities involving computer-based testing include paper-and-pencil testing, with the recording of the responses on an optical mark scan form or sheets. At the end of the testing period, the individual scan sheets are collected; they are read into the computer at a later time.

Test Scoring

Test scoring by computer is accomplished by matching a student's response for each item with the correct response recorded for that item in the test key. The computer is programmed to make a correct or incorrect decision based on the match between the answer in the test key and the student's answer. However, the more open-ended the response becomes, the more complex the computer's task. True-false, multiple-choice, and matching questions are easily handled because the answer is finite and specific and can be expressed in a precise number or letter. Fill-in-the-blank, short-answer, and essay questions become much more difficult to include because decisions must be made about the specific nature of the response in order to be calculated as correct.

During the 1986–1987 school year, the testing component of an instructional management system we described in chapter 4 was used to facilitate the testing of language arts skills. To evaluate student progress and assess student abilities in language arts, the unit tests accompanying the Scott, Foresman basal reading series (Aaron et al., 1981) were used in coordination with the computer-based testing system.

Creating a Test Key. Before a test can be scored, a test key must be established in the program to identity each test item (usually by number), the correct response for the item, and the instructional objective the item is linked with. In the application at the Oak Grove Elementary School, test keys were established to correlate with the unit tests that accompany the Scott, Foresman reading system. To establish a test key, most computer-based testing programs include the following procedures.

1. Name the test (or test key).
2. Identify the objective to which you will be linking a test item or items.
3. Indicate the item number.

4. Indicate the correct answer.

5. Repeat this procedure for every item until test key is completed.

In the illustration in Figure 5.3 the steps in creating a test key for the Scott–Foresman Hidden Wonders test are shown.

Usually the scoring process takes place immediately and automatically as the computer receives the student's responses. As the scores are entered, either through keyboard entry, use of an optical scanner, or as a result of taking the test directly on the computer, each student's responses are matched with the correct responses in the test key.

Test Interpretation

After teacher Betty Coburn has developed, administered, and scored a test, she must interpret the results. If the purpose for giving the test was to evaluate the progress of the students in the class and to assign grades for feedback to them, the scores the students earned must be translated into grades. This process, though time consuming and tedious, is usually a rather simple computational activity. However, if the purpose of the testing was to provide information for instructional planning for a student in her class, for example, who seems to be quite bright but is falling behind academically, Betty Coburn will need to interpret the pattern of the raw scores as well as their values and make judgments about the student's academic strengths and weaknesses. In addition, she will want to make decisions about the best instructional methods and procedures to use with the student, based on information gained from the testing.

The complexity of test interpretation will vary, depending on the purpose for the testing (see Table 5.1). The use of computers to assist with test interpretations can be divided into these same categories: (1) student evaluation—to change raw scores into grades (or other relative standing indicators such as percentiles or grade equivalencies), (2) educational assessment—to develop instructional plans based on the test results and personal characteristics of the student, and/or (3) diagnosis—to make classification decisions about educational placement.

Computations and Assignment of Grades

Most teachers develop and administer tests to evaluate the progress of the students in the class and to assign grades. Assigning grades to students involves translating the raw scores each student earns into grades. Most teacher-made tests, as well as many supplied by testing and textbook companies, are scored on a criterion basis. That is, an absolute range of scores is established to correspond to each grade level, such as scores of 90–100=A, 80–89=B, 70–79=C, 60–69=D, 59 and below=F. Many

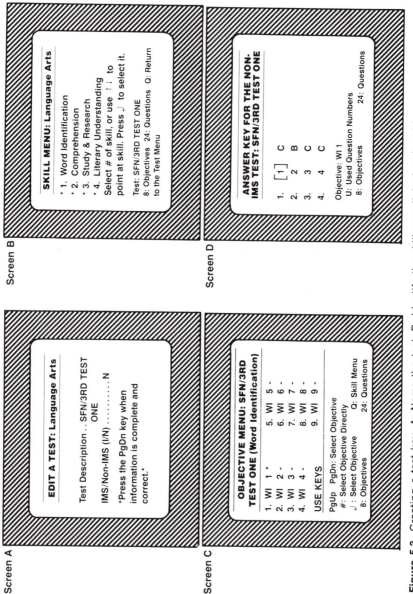

Screen A

> **EDIT A TEST: Language Arts**
>
> Test Description . . SFN/3RD TEST ONE
>
> IMS/Non-IMS (I/N) . . . . N
>
> *Press the PgDn key when information is complete and correct.*

Screen B

> **SKILL MENU: Language Arts**
>
> * 1. Word Identification
> * 2. Comprehension
> * 3. Study & Research
> * 4. Literary Understanding
>
> Select # of skill, or use ↑↓ to point at skill. Press ↵ to select it.
>
> Test: SFN/3RD TEST ONE
> 8: Objectives 24: Questions Q: Return to the Test Menu

Screen C

> **OBJECTIVE MENU: SFN/3RD TEST ONE (Word Identification)**
>
> 1. WI 1 *   5. WI 5 -
> 2. WI 2 -   6. WI 6 -
> 3. WI 3 -   7. WI 7 -
> 4. WI 4 -   8. WI 8 -
>   9. WI 9 -
>
> USE KEYS
>
> PgUp PgDn: Select Objective
> #: Select Objective Directly
> ↵: Select Objective   Q: Skill Menu
> 8: Objectives   24: Questions

Screen D

> **ANSWER KEY FOR THE NON-IMS TEST: SFN/3RD TEST ONE**
>
> 1. [1] C
> 2.   2   B
> 3.   3   C
> 4.   4   C
>
> Objective: WI 1
> U: Used Question Numbers
> 8: Objectives   24: Questions

Figure 5.3. Creating a test key. A: Name the test. B: Identify the skill area linked to item(s). C: Identify objectives linked to items. D: Indicate the item number and correct answer.

106

testing software programs allow you to indicate your grading criteria by entering that information into the computer. Once you have specified the grading parameters and raw scores have been entered for a group of students, the computer program takes over. The program will translate the raw scores earned by each student into a grade.

Although most testing software programs available for use at the local level will compute grades based on the teacher's criteria, few provide interpretation of progress in relationship to instructional objectives. Most of the large, standardized testing companies, however, use computer-based testing programs that compute standard scores and percentile standings as well as grade equivalency scores.

Figure 5.4 presents a printed report generated from the CompuScore software program published by DLM-Teaching Resources Corporation. CompuScore is used to assist with the scoring of the Woodcock-Johnson Psycho-Educational Battery (Woodcock, 1978), an individual achievement test. The Woodcock-Johnson has twenty-seven subtests, including tests of cognitive ability, academic achievement, and interests. The program is simple to use. The total raw score for each subtest (e.g., Word Attack) is entered into the program, the user following directions on the screen and using the keyboard. Based on the raw scores entered for an individual student, a series of interpretive scores are calculated and printed in a report for the student. As can be seen in Figure 5.4, several types of scores, including grade scores and standard scores, are calculated. A judgment of functional level is also indicated. For example, Jonathan McCreadie, the subject of this test-scoring report is mildly delayed (MD) in reading but is high average (HA) in written language ability. These calculations could be made by hand, using the score conversion tables in the manual of the test. However, manual calculations will take three to four times longer, with a greater chance of human error.

As the use of computers becomes more widespread, the number of score interpretation and grading programs available are increasing. Examples of grading programs available for use include MicroGrade (Chariot Software Group, 1986), Micro Test Administration System (Science Research Associates, 1985), Autoscor (Cognitronics Corporation, 1985), and The Teacher's Gradebook (Dynacomp, Inc., 1984).

A series of well-known software programs that translate raw scores into more interpretable scores and data are published by American Guidance Services to support tests that they publish (ASSIST programs for the Kaufman Assessment Battery for Children, Woodcock Reading Mastery Tests, and the Peabody Individual Achievement Test). Educators interested in gaining more information about the various testing-related software programs available commercially should review a copy of the latest *Psychware* courseware reference manual (Krug, 1987).

Figure 5.4. Test results computation report. Reprinted by permision of the publisher.

Compuscore for the Woodcock-Johnson Psycho-Educational Battery
PUBLISHED BY DLM TEACHING RESOURCES—PROGRAMMED BY JAY HAUGER

NAME: Jonathan McCreadie **GRADE:** 6.3 **BIRTHDATE:** 12/12/1975 **SEX:** M

EXAMINER: David Jones   **TEST DATE:** 10/18/1987   **AGE:** 11 Yrs 10 Mos

SCHOOL/AGENCY: Kingston Public Schools **CITY:** Kingston **STATE:** NC

RAW SCORES:

INSTRUCTIONS:
1. **Verify raw scores against the raw scores in the response booklets**
2. **Plot confidence bands on the subtest profiles**
3. **Plot vertical lines on the subtest profiles:**
   Cognitive Ability = 501
   Sum of Achievement = 1904
   Sum of Interest = 1007

1. 18	6. 17	11. 27	16. 7	S. 34	23. 19
2. 23	7. 15	12. 17	17. 5	U. 5	24. 14
3. 15	8. 25	13. 19	18. 23	20. 21	25. 20
4. 21	9. 14	14. 23	19. 18	21. 5	26. 16
5. 21	10. 21	15. 19	P. 12	22. 20	27. 17

COMPUTER-ASSISTED TEST INTERPRETATION

Computers are frequently used to assist with the development of inter-pretive reports that are used for instructional planning. Interpretive reporting is one of the more difficult tasks that the computer undertakes in assisting with testing procedures. Most of the difficulty with computer-assisted interpretation of tests is related to the subjectivity of test interpretation itself and has nothing to do with the power and capabilities of the computer. This problem is much more evident in interpretations of the results of aptitude (i.e., IQ) and personality tests than it is in interpretations involving the results of educational achievement tests.

Most test interpretation software programs rely on a series of IF-THEN statements in the computer program that establish the rules for decision making. That is, IF a certain value or score is obtained (or a

Figure 5.4. (Continued)

CLUSTER ANALYSIS BY AGE

INSTRUCTIONS:

If age comparisons are desired, plot the following percentile rank ranges on the response booklet profile.

	CLUSTER SCORE	AGE SCORE	DIFF SCORE	STAN SCORE	AGE PR		PR RANGE	RPI (AGE)	FUNC LEVEL
FS BROAD COG ABIL	501	10-3	-8	89	23	18	28	79/90	LA
PRE/SHORT BROAD COG	498	9-10	-10	87	20	15	27	75/90	LA
BRIEF COG ABIL	495	9-6	-21	81	10	6	15	47/90	MD
VERBAL ABILITY	515	12-0	1	101	53	40	65	91/90	A
ORAL LANGUAGE	504	10-8	-7	92	31	22	42	81/90	LA
REASONING	498	9-7	-8	92	30	18	42	79/90	LA
BROAD REASONING	502	10-8	-6	92	30	22	38	82/90	LA
VISUAL-PERC SPEED	480	8-4	-34	72	3	1	6	18/90	SD
MEMORY	570	36/95	64	163	99	99	99	100/90	VS
READING APTITUDE	510	X	1	102	56	41	64	X	X
MATHEMATICS APTITUDE	500	X	-12	86	17	12	24	X	X
WR LANGUAGE APTITUDE	496	X	-19	81	10	7	15	X	X
KNOWLEDGE APTITUDE	500	X	-13	87	20	16	26	X	X
READING	490	8-10	-24	83	13	11	17	39/90	MD
MATHEMATICS	419	6-0	-99	20	1	1	1	0/90	SD
WRITTEN LANGUAGE	525	13-0	6	106	66	54	76	95/90	HA
KNOWLEDGE	470	7-1	-40	66	1	1	2	10/90	SD
SKILLS	449	7-0	-69	49	1	1	1	0/90	SD
SCHOLASTIC INT	512	X	14	121	92	88	94	98/90	HA
NONSCHOLASTIC INT	495	X	-6	89	23	14	35	82/90	LA

value within a range of values is obtained) THEN the computer is directed to get a specific set of information to include in the report. This information can be a paragraph or a sentence describing characteristics of the student, or it may be a list of suggested instructional activities to use with the student. In the more powerful computer programs, a series of interrelated and conditional IF-THEN statements can be used to interpret a variety of test scores (as well as personal variables such as age) to narrow the response selected to highly specific prescriptive information. The responses are placed together in a prearranged sequence that forms the interpretive report. For example, let's say that items 4, 5, 6, 8, 9, 11, and 12 on a test all measure a student's ability to recognize and pronounce three-letter blends. If the student is six years old and correctly answers four out of the seven items, a statement indicating that the student is "doing very well for his or her age" can be located and printed. On the other hand, if the student is fourteen years old and correctly answers four out of seven items, a statement indicating that "the student is having difficulty with three-letter blends and remediation instruction should be initiated" would be located and printed. Furthermore, the program could have a feature that will locate appropriate instructional activities to be used with the student.

Figure 5.5 shows a section of basic code from the Unistar II+ (Lillie & Edwards, 1986b) software program used to generate individual educational plans for exceptional children. In the figure, the program commands link a series of grade equivalency (GE) score ranges with statements that are located in another part of the program code. Line 92, for example, indicates that IF the GE score entered is greater than 2.4 and less than 2.7, THEN the program will go to line 129 to receive directions to print a specific statement—in this case a series of instructional objectives that have been correlated with the range of GE scores.

A more efficient and acceptable approach to linking test results to prescriptive instructional information is employed when specific responses to test items are linked directly to prescriptive statements. A number of programs have been developed to analyze the information derived from the errors or incorrect responses to specific test items. Some of the most advanced developments in error analysis have evolved through the use of expert systems. Brown and Burton (1978) developed a computerized system called Buggy for training teachers in spelling diagnostic skills. Using similar logic, researchers at the Xerox Palo Alto Research Center have developed an error analysis system, Debuggy, dealing specifically with place value subtraction (Harmon & King, 1985).

```
LIST88,100

88    IF GE  >  =  0.4 AND GE  <  =  0.7 THEN   GOTO 125
89    IF GE  >  =  0.8 AND GE  <  =  1.3 THEN   GOTO 126
90    IF GE  >  =  1.4 AND GE  <  =  1.7 THEN   GOTO 127
91    IF GE  >  =  1.8 AND GE  <  =  2.3 THEN   GOTO 128
92    IF GE  >  =  2.4 AND GE  <  =  2.7 THEN   GOTO 129
93    IF GE  >  =  2.8 AND GE  <  =  3.3 THEN   GOTO 130
94    IF GE  >  =  3.4 AND GE  <  =  3.7 THEN   GOTO 131
95    IF GE  >  =  3.8 AND GE  <  =  4.3 THEN   GOTO 132
96    IF GE  >  =  4.4 AND GE  <  =  4.7 THEN   GOTO 133
97    IF GE  >  =  4.8 AND GE  <  =  5.3 THEN   GOTO 134
98    IF GE  >  =  5.4 AND GE  <  =  5.7 THEN   GOTO 135
99    IF GE  >  =  5.8 AND GE  <  =  6.3 THEN   GOTO 136
100   GOSUB 175: POKE 54,0: POKE 55,193: PRINT CHR$ (9); "80N": IF P5 = 0
      THEN PRINT "Goals & Objectives are not included at this level.": PRINT :PR#
      0:LP = LP + 3
```

Figure 5.5. Section of BASIC code designed to interpret test results

The program conducts an elaborate analysis of the procedures a student uses in solving subtraction problems. First, the student works on solving a series of problems. The program matches the student's procedures and solutions with a large set of "bugs," common errors that students make when subtracting. The program then attempts to explain the student's "subtraction behavior" with the use of an internal set of rules established in the program. Once the program has identified the rules that the student is having difficulty with, it checks out its hypotheses by generated subtraction problems that test the student's understanding of these rules. If the rule check confirms the type of bug (or more probably bugs) that are present in the student's problem-solving behavior, the program initiates practice exercises to eliminate the problem.

A generic error analysis program developed by Lillie and Edwards (1987) allows the user to establish the decision-making parameters for conducting an error analysis for a specific test. This program operates very much like an instructional management system. A *prescription key* is developed by the teacher or psychologist, linking combinations of missed items on a test with specific suggestions for remediation and/or instruction.

Diagnostic Classification

Diagnostic testing is big business in the United States today, particularly as it relates to the identification and placement of students into specific special educational programs. Schools are very actively involved in decision making to classify students as learning disabled, emotionally disturbed, educable mentally handicapped, speech and language impaired, trainable mentally handicapped, or multihandicapped. The classification process is primarily tied to administrative and legal responsibilities of the schools in relationship to establishing and funding special instructional programs for exceptional and/or handicapped students.

The technical process the computer uses in conducting interpretations that result in information to make classification decisions is very similar to the process used in other interpretation tasks. However, using test interpretation programs for diagnostic decision making can be a risky business. Diagnostic interpretations of test scores contain decision-making rules that rely on clinical expertise, which is subjective and difficult to reproduce through a computer program. The decision-making process is not nearly as objective as it is in the computation of grades based on raw scores from a test. Instructional planning decisions are also more objective than classification decisions. These linkages are direct matches between the student's abilities and specific instructional objectives within the curricular scope and sequence. In other words, the decision-making process is fairly well defined when the results of a criterion referenced achievement test are used to make decisions about instructional content. This is not the case, however, when individual intelligence and/or other diagnostic tests are used to make clinical decisions pertaining to a specific educational or psychological classification.

Nevertheless, there are a number of widely used interpretive software programs that emulate the diagnostic decision-making process of "expert diagnosticians." Diagnostic report writing software programs are available for many of the widely used individual intelligence, personality, interests, and aptitude tests, including programs for the Wechsler Intelligence Scale for Children–Revised (WISC-R), Wechsler Intelligence Scale for Adults, Slosson Intelligence, Stanford-Binet Intelligence Test, Rorschach Projective Test, and Minnesota Multiphasic Personality Inventory. A quick review of the *Psychware Sourcebook* (Krug, 1987) will identify over 300 computer-based assessment programs, most of which produce a diagnostic report. Figure 5.6, pages 114–115, illustrates a portion of a report generated with a WISC-R Report diagnostic interpretation program. The publishers take care to report that the program was designed by qualified behavioral scientists utilizing well-validated clinical research, and that no diagnostic or classification decision should be made solely upon the contents of the report.

Most professionals agree that computer-based diagnostic reports should be used as a part of a decision support system. That is, the computer-generated diagnostic report provides additional information, or a second opinion, for the diagnostician to consider and, if warranted, integrate with other clinical information to make a final decision. However, most programs advise against relying totally on interpretive reports produced by the program.

The use of computers for test analysis and interpretation is extensively related to the developing computer technology area of expert systems.

Expert Systems. Although computer programs are becoming better at emulating expert judgment, as indicated earlier, reducing complicated diagnostic decision making to a series of specific, well-defined measurable statements tends to oversimplify the diagnostic process.

According to many specialists in computer technology, the use of computers to provide expert systems across many fields of knowledge will be one of the major contributions of computer technology (Harmon & King, 1985). Expert systems may make it possible for teachers and administrators to develop quick, high-level answers to a wide range of educational problems. An area of education that seems to be readily applicable to the use of expert systems is test analysis and interpretation.

Many clinical and school psychologists have spent many years accumulating knowledge about the interpretation of psychological and academic tests administered in schools. Most teachers and educators do not have that knowledge or experiential background. Ideally, after giving an individual test, or receiving the score from an examiner, a teacher would ask an expert on the interpretation of that test how he or she would interpret these results. With the use of an expert system designed for test interpretation, teachers can "talk" with an "in-residence" specialist to get advice on how to interpret a particular set of scores or responses. In addition, the latest, more elaborate expert systems are designed to allow for quick updates of the information in residence in the system. This capability allows expert systems to keep pace with new knowledge on a specific topic.

The developing field of expert systems has grown out of the work in artificial intelligence. *Artificial intelligence* is usually defined in general terms as "the study of how to make computers do things at which, at the moment, people are better" (Rich, 1983). In the field of artificial intelligence, there are three major areas of research and development which are frequently referred to as natural language processing, robotics, and expert systems. Natural language processing is primarily concerned with developing application software that will allow the computer to read, speak, or understand language as people use it in conversation. Robotics development is concerned with the use of smart robots to perform tasks based on visual, auditory, and tactile information perceived by the robot. The incoming information that the robot is interpreting and reacting to changes as the robot moves around the environment. The third area is concerned with developing programs that use symbolic knowledge to simulate the behavior of human experts (Harmon & King, 1985).

The application of expert system technology to educational and psychological testing is still very much in its infancy. Many computer technology specialists would classify the current attempts in this area as very crude efforts at building expert systems (if they classified them as expert systems at all). Conversely, many professionals in psychological and educational testing view the use of computer technology to generate diagnostic reports with alarm. They believe that clinical test interpretation is an individual, heuristic effort that can be duplicated by a computer only in a very shallow, and perhaps even in an unprofessional, manner.

However, the use of expert systems in education holds a great deal of promise. Applications that are available at this time, though limited in design, can be helpful if used with discretion. The important point is that the technology exists to build a variety of expert systems to perform a variety of tasks in education. If the resulting expert system programs are shallow and lack professional integrity, it is not the fault of the technology but rather the lack of expert use of the technology.

Figure 5.6. WISC-R Report (Wechsler Intelligence Scale for Children—Revised). Copyright © 1974 by the Psychological Corporation. Reproduced by permision. All rights reserved.

Name: John X. Doe
Sex: male
School: Anytown School
Grade: 3

Date of Test: 02-27-84
Date of Birth: 11-01-75
Race: Caucasian
Examiner: John Q. Smith Ph.D.

Current Placement: regular classes
Reason For Referral: behavioral problems

SUBTEST SCALED SCORES

Information	12	Picture Completion	13
Similarities	4	Picture Arrangement	14
Arithmetic	12	Block Design	14
Vocabulary	9	Object Assembly	16
Comprehension	15	Coding	9
Digit Span	11	Mazes	9

Verbal Scale IQ Score   102
Performance Scale IQ Score   123
Full Scale IQ Score   112   (79%ile)

BEHAVIORAL OBSERVATIONS:

John Doe is an 8-year-old Caucasian male who was referred because of behavioral problems. He is a blonde haired, blue eyed person of average height and average body build. At the time of testing, John presented an overall neat appearance. Dress was appropriate and he was generally well groomed.

John's performance on the tasks indicates he is left hand dominant. During the session, some speech problems, no obvious sensory visual difficulty, and no obvious hearing difficulty were observed. He exhibited appropriate skill with gross motor movements and age-appropriate skill with fine motor movements. Activity level was generally overly active.

Rapport with John was easily established. He was socially confident and comfortable in his interactions and talked to the examiner freely. John generally understood instructions readily. He exhibited an overall indifferent attitude towards the evaluation and motivation was variable across tasks. His approach to assessment tasks was impulsive and poorly planned. He preferred only easy items. Concentration was erratic. He gave up too quickly. Praise had no observable effect. He overreacted to errors/failures and became self-critical or angry. No unusual or bizarre behaviors were observed during the session. In general this is believed to be an accurate estimate of John's current level of intellectual functioning.

Figure 5.6. (Continued)

INTELLIGENCE AND FACTOR QUOTIENTS:

On this administration of the Wechsler Intelligence Scale for Children—Revised, John obtained a Verbal Scale IQ score of 102 and a Performance Scale IQ score of 123. This results in a Full Scale IQ score of 112 which falls within the High Average range of intellectual abilities. The Full Scale IQ score corresponds to the 79%ile which indicates he is functioning intellectually at a level equal to or better than approximately 79% of the children the same age. Overall, John performed significantly poorer on items tapping verbal comprehension skills than he did on tasks requiring perceptual organization. The ability to attend to, concentrate on, and manipulate numerical material, may interfere with optimal performance and is significantly below perceptual organization skills.

Based on the present results, there is a 90% probability that John's true level of overall intellectual functioning falls in the range of 106 to 116. If he is retested at a later date, the chances are 90 out of 100 that he will obtain a Full Scale IQ score in the range of 104 to 118, unless there have been factors which have resulted in significant changes in his true level of functioning.

SUBTEST PATTERNS:

Examination of John's performance across the different subtests indicates he exhibited a pattern of strength on subtests tapping social judgment. A particular pattern of weakness was exhibited on subtests that tend to tap learning ability, and on tasks tapping visual memory.

VERBAL COMPREHENSION:

John's performance on verbally-related material falls in the Average range and corresponds to the 55%ile. There was significant variability in his performance across the different subtests and achieved levels fell in the Mentally Retarded to Superior range.

In comparison to John's overall performance on verbal comprehension items, he exhibited relative strength on subtests measuring:
  **judgment and common sense; practical information plus ability to evaluate and use past experience
Significant relative weaknesses on the verbal items were evidenced on subtests tapping:
  **logical abstractive (categorical) thinking

PERCEPTUAL ORGANIZATION:

John's performance on tasks requiring perceptual organization and visual-motor skills falls in the Superior range and corresponds to the 94%ile. There was substantial variability in his performance across the different subtests and achieved levels fell in the Average to Very Superior range.

Performance on perceptual organization subtests did not indicate any significant relative strengths.

Oak Grove Elementary School
SCORING REPORT—SFN/3RD/TEST 1 PRETEST

Today's Date: 01-01-1980   ** = 100

		Objectives							
		W I .1	W I .5	W I .6	R C .1	R C .9	R C .15	S R .3	S R .4
No. Questions	24	4	2	2	4	2	2	4	4
ID CODE					% of Questions Correct				
850713	83	**	50	**	75	50	**	**	75
860103	79	75	**	**	75	**	50	75	75
840484	79	**	50	50	75	**	**	75	75
830493	91	**	**	**	75	50	**	**	**
830322	58	25	50	**	75	50	50	75	50
850538	66	50	50	**	75	**	0	75	75
860560	68	50	**	**	50	**	50	50	50
840055	91	**	50	50	**	**	**	**	**
850516	100	**	**	**	**	**	**	**	**
830316	58	75	**	0	75	0	50	75	50
880177	68	75	50	50	85	**	**	50	75
Average %	75	77	72	77	78	77	73	73	75

Figure 5.7. Sample test results report

Although the use of computer-based diagnostic expert systems in the field of medical diagnosis is increasing rapidly, diagnostic applications in education are at the infancy level. Education will have to overcome some inherent difficulties in the complexity of educational diagnosis, combined with a relatively shallow knowledge base. The relationships between diagnostic testing and appropriate treatments are not as well documented and/or defined in education as they are in the more scientifically based field of medicine. Consequently, computer-based diagnosis is not developing as rapidly in education as it is in some other disciplines.

Item Analysis

A few of the testing software programs available also provide the capability to conduct an item analysis to evaluate the quality of each item on a test. An item analysis involves an examination of the pattern of

Oak Grove Elementary School

TEST ITEMS MISSED—SFN/3RD/TEST 1 PRETEST

Today's Date: 01-01-1980

Page 1
(** = 100)

Question Number	1	2	3	4	5	6	7	8	9	10	11	12	13	14	15	16	17	18	19	20
850713						x		x					x							
860103		x											x		x					x
840484					x		x							x						x
830492							x							x						
830300	x	x		x		x		x					x	x						x
850538		x	x			x		x					x		x	x				
860560		x	x										x	x	x		x			x
840055					x		x													
850516																				
830316	x			x	x			x	x				x		x					x
880177				x		x	x	x					x	x	x			x	x	

———————— Students Missing Each Question ————————

	1	2	3	4	5	6	7	8	9	10	11	12	13	14	15	16	17	18	19	20
Total Number	2	4	8	2	1	4	2	6	1	4	0	1	7	4	3	3	2	1	1	5
Total Percentage	18	38	18	18	9	36	0	54	9	36	0	9	63	35	27	37	18	9	8	45
Total Students	11																			

Figure 5.7. (Continued)

responses for each item across students who have responded to the item. Usually an item analysis looks at two main aspects of test items—item difficulty and item discrimination ability. Item difficulty can be calculated by simply tracking the percentage of students correctly responding to the item. Discrimination ability compares the percentage of high-scoring students who pass the item with the percentage of low-scoring students who pass the item. Different item analysis programs use different criteria for determining which students are to be included in each of these groups. For teachers and/or schools that use the same criterion referenced tests once or twice each year, an item analysis feature can be extremely helpful in improving the quality of the tests.

MONITORING AND REPORTING

As we discussed in chapter 2, frequent monitoring and timely feedback to students is a very important feature in effective instructional practices. Almost all the testing software programs available provide printed reports that can be used to report to students, as well as reports that can be used to report to parents if desired. Most program reports include raw score, percentage of items correct, and percentile score for each student. Some reports include which items were missed or passed and objective mastery as well. In addition, many programs will calculate and report class or group information. These reports may include the percentage of students who passed each item on the test, class average, and range of scores. Figure 5.7 illustrates two reports from an instructional management system that includes testing features.

SUMMARY

The measurement of student achievement and progress is a very significant aspect of American education. As the demand for accountability in the nation's schools increases, the time, energy, and money spent on evaluation of student achievement increases. Today, teachers find themselves extensively involved in developing, administering, scoring, and reporting the results of tests. This chapter has presented information on the use of computers to assist educators with testing-related tasks and activities. Although computer-assisted testing programs are primarily limited to objective, multiple-choice, or true-false tests, there remain a number of benefits in using such programs. Teachers can decrease the amount of time they spend on testing related activities as well as improve the accuracy of test scoring. In addition, computer-assisted testing can greatly facilitate proven approaches to individualized instruction such as mastery learning.

To facilitate the development of criterion referenced tests, computer-based test item banks can be developed and used to construct tests. Test item banks are computer files that contain test items correlated with the instructional objectives they are designed to measure. Tests can be constructed by the selection of items from the test item bank. Once constructed, tests can be administered in several ways. Some programs allow students to take a multiple-choice test directly on the computer, frequently referred to as *on-line* testing. In actual practice, however, tests are usually administered in the traditional paper-and-pencil fashion, on an optical scan sheet, with results entered into the computer by an optical scanning device.

The speed and accuracy with which computer-assisted testing programs can score and interpret tests can greatly improve the efficiency of achievement as well as diagnostic testing. On the negative side, if the diagnostic or interpretive decision-making rules residing in the program are inaccurate or inappropriate, the computer-assisted diagnostic program will merely make bad decisions faster. Hence, the value of interpretive diagnostic computer-assisted testing programs depends on the validity of the decision-making rules incorporated into the program.

Used with judgment, computer-assisted student assessment can greatly facilitate several of the effective teaching practices discussed in chapter 2, including frequent and routine checking of student performance and frequent and sustained instructional feedback to the students.

PUTTING THE BOOK TO WORK

To help you review and summarize this chapter, fourteen questions follow. Read each question and briefly review the source pages indicated. Write a response for each question.

Question	*Source*
1. How can computers help teachers reduce the amount of time that they spend on testing tasks?	92–93
2. For what different purposes are tests administered in elementary and secondary schools?	93–94
3. What is a computer-based test item bank?	96–99
4. How does a test item bank facilitate the development of tests?	96–99
5. How is an optical scanner used to facilitate computer-based testing?	100–101
6. What are some advantages and disadvantages in using optical scanners for scoring tests?	100–101
7. What does "on-line" testing refer to?	102–104
8. What are some advantages and disadvantages to on-line testing?	102–104
9. Why is a test key an important concept in computer-based testing?	104–105
10. What are the three main types of computer-based test interpretation programs and how are they different?	105–108
11. What major issues are involved with the use of computer-based diagnostic report-writing programs?	111–112
12. What are IF-THEN statements and how are they used in some computer-based test interpretation programs?	108–110
13. Which effective teaching principles discussed in chapter 2 are facilitated with the use of computer-based testing programs?	92–94
14. What are expert systems and how do they relate to computer-based testing?	112–113

CHAPTER 6

Special Learners and Special Applications

Objectives

When you have read this chapter, you should be able to do the following:

1. Describe an information-processing learning model and compare it to how computers operate and/or function.

2. Identify the specific learning characteristics that may be displayed by students who are having learning difficulties.

3. Identify CBI courseware features that can facilitate the instruction of students with visual impairments.

4. Identify CBI courseware features that can facilitate the instruction of students with hearing impairments.

5. Identify CBI courseware features that can facilitate the instruction of students who are having difficulties focusing attention on the learning task.

6. Identify CBI courseware features that can facilitate the instruction of students who demonstrate organization and/or memory problems.

7. Identify CBI courseware features that can facilitate the instruction of students who demonstrate expressive language difficulties.

8. Identify CBI courseware features that can facilitate the development of higher-order computer skills.
9. Identify and compare three types of authoring tools.

INTRODUCTION: SPECIAL LEARNERS IN TODAY'S CLASSROOM

Although the red brick, one-room schoolhouse may have disappeared from the American educational scene, individual differences among students in the typical public school classroom are as numerous as ever. During the first three-quarters of the twentieth century, most students with special learning problems were identified and placed in separate special education classrooms or schools. Today, however, more than 80 percent of the students identified as having special educational needs spend more time in regular classrooms than in special classrooms. As a result, the typical teacher is confronted with a diverse group of students, with an array of different learning problems and handicaps.

Earlier, we introduced Betty Coburn, a teacher of a somewhat special third-grade class. Let's take a closer look at that class. Betty Coburn has a total of twenty-eight students. One student is seriously visually impaired and needs modifications in visual materials for most of his instructional activities. Two other students have been diagnosed as having a specific learning disability. Although they receive one period a day of specialized instruction in a resource room, the two learning-disabled children are in Betty Coburn's classroom during the other five periods each day. Another four children are achieving significantly below grade level, to the extent that they qualify for federal government Title I services for high-risk students. The program provides additional reading instruction for the four children outside the third-grade classroom, but these four children still receive more than 80 percent of their instruction from Betty Coburn.

It is clear to most classroom teachers that the diversity of abilities and learning characteristics of their students presents a huge challenge to the skills of the teachers. In many instances, the effective instruction principles discussed in chapter 2 must be implemented on an individual basis. Although the principles do not change for children with special instructional needs, careful planning is needed to ensure that these principles are operating on a daily basis. The purpose of this chapter is to provide you with an understanding of the effective use of computers for instruction of students with exceptional, or different, learning needs. This information should enable you to make informed decisions about the use of computers for various types of special needs students.

INFORMATION PROCESSING, COMPUTERS, AND LEARNING

To look at an individual student in terms of his or her abilities to learn, we must first establish a learning theory framework within which to organize learning abilities and disabilities. One of the most widely accepted views of how humans learn is represented by the information-processing model of learning. Although there are several variations, all information-processing learning models have similar elements. This model is very appropriate for discussion in a text on the use of computers in instruction because it resembles the computers as a model for human learning. People learn in very much the same way as computers process information. This process involves a sequence of (1) receiving information; (2) retaining, retrieving, and processing information; and (3) responding. The computer analogy is clear—the computer receives information through the keyboard, various types of scanners, or a modem. The computer retains the information in its memory and, if directed, processes the information with the aid of an executive controlling mechanism, usually referred to as the software program. Computer responses (or output) are usually presented through information on the monitor screen or by sending information to a printer.

When a student is having difficulty with various learning tasks, one approach to diagnosing, remediating, and/or compensating for the problem is to determine where, within the information-processing system, the problem is occurring. Figure 6.1 is an illustration of a typical information-processing model, adapted from Gagne's work in instructional theory (1985).

Within each of the basic components of the information-processing learning model in Figure 6.1, we have listed some characteristics that are frequently found in students with various learning difficulties. From the environment, a student receives stimulation through the *receptors,* or the senses of vision, hearing, touch, and smell. A student with a vision or hearing disability obviously will have difficulties at this stage of the learning process. Physically disabled students, such as a child with multiple sclerosis, may also have problems at this stage.

In Gagne's rendition of an information-processing learning model, the stimulus flows from the *receptor* to the *sensory registor,* where it stays for only a brief interval. Learning problems that might affect the quality of the processing of information at this level include poor visual perceptual abilities, poor motor coordination, and/or problems with selective attention. Selective attention refers to the process of selecting and transforming perceived stimuli into a meaningful form for storage in short-term memory.

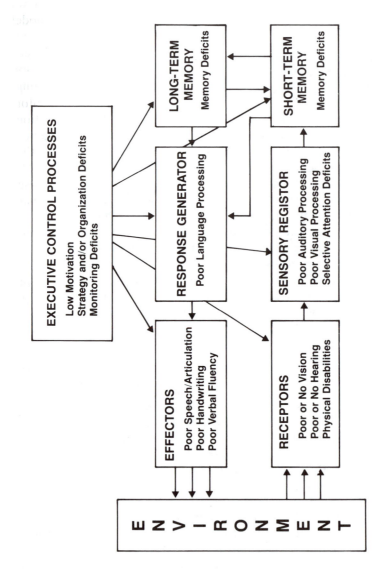

Figure 6.1. Information-processing learning model and learning problems. (Adapted from *The conditions of learning and theory of instruction*, Fourth Edition, by R. M. Gagne, 1988, p. 71. New York: Holt, Rinehart & Winston.)

In short-term memory, prominent features of the original stimulation are stored. According to Gagne (1985), short-term memory has a limited capacity for the amount of information that can be contained and engaged in at any one time. As new information is rehearsed in short-term memory, it is meaningfully coded. This process, labeled *semantic encoding* by Gagne, prepares information for transfer and storage in long-term memory.

The process of semantic encoding and transferring of information from short-term memory to long-term memory is a very important part of learning and frequently breaks down in some students, resulting in learning difficulties. These students demonstrate disorganization and lack strategies for meaningfully coding new information relative to their currently coded information in long-term memory.

Once information is semantically coded and residing in long-term memory, a process of searching and retrieving information takes place within the *response generator* phase. During this phase, information is selected and organized for a response. Finally, through the *effectors* phase, the student undertakes the physical act of responding. In schools, this response is likely to be in the form of written expression (writing), verbal expression (speaking), or physical action. This brief review of an information-processing model of learning has been presented to establish a framework to help us think about the application and use of computers for instruction of students with various types of learning problems. For a more detailed discussion of the information-processing learning model and its application to learning and instruction, we recommend that you read *The Conditions of Learning* (Gagne, 1985), and *Principles of Instructional Design* (Gagne, Briggs, & Wager, 1988).

SPECIAL POPULATIONS IN THE SCHOOLS

Providing appropriate instructional services to qualified exceptional students is an important aspect of American education. The terms *exceptional children* and *special education* are associated with students who, because of their mental, emotional, social, sensory, physical, or communication gifts or disabilities, require specially planned and implemented instructional programs to provide them with an appropriate education. A number of different special label categories are frequently used when discussing special needs students. Most of these categories are incorporated under provisions for special education instructional services in state and federal laws. These categories include specific learning disabilities, emotional and behavioral disorders, mentally handicapped, visually impaired, hearing impaired, speech and language disorders, physically handicapped, and gifted and talented. Also, a category of "high-risk" students is frequently employed when considering the delivery of additional instructional services. The high-risk category, however, is not considered a special education category for classification and funding purposes. For a detailed discussion of exceptional children, a number of texts are available (such as Berdine & Blackhurst, 1986; Kirk & Gallagher, 1986).

Through the years, the categories used in identifying and labeling students for participation in special education programs have proven to be valuable in providing badly needed educational services and funds. On the negative side, the special education classifications have not been very helpful in planning and implementing specific instructional procedures for individual students within each category. When planning specific individual instructional programs and activities, educators have found it much more fruitful to concentrate on specific learning characteristics of students within, as well as across, the specific classification designations. For example, children with specific learning disabilities (SLD) are frequently found to have attention deficits. However, not all students classified as SLD have attention deficits. Conversely, not all children with attention deficits should be classified as having a specific learning disability. For instructional planning purposes, it is much more productive to identify a student's strengths and weaknesses in terms of specific learning characteristics that can be linked to instructional practices.

Table 6.1 presents the specific learning characteristics that are usually associated with the various classifications of exceptional students. The characteristics are grouped under (1) cognitive domain; (2) affective domain; and (3) a hybrid domain including abilities and disabilities in the motor, sensory, and physical domains. Although a number of the learning characteristics can be found across several categories, Table 6.1 lists the major characteristics found within each category. As can be seen, the characteristics, or problems, identified do not exclusively belong to any one classification category.

The columns on the right side of Table 6.1 indicate the type of contribution possible with computer applications. The CBI column refers to the potential for a significant contribution with the use of computer-based instruction. The compensatory column refers to the use of computers to take the place of or compensate for, ability deficiencies resulting from a handicap. As indicated in the third column, students with all kinds of learning problems can benefit from instruction that is structured and managed through the use of computer-based instructional management systems.

A teacher must be aware of the specific learning characteristics of each student in his or her class. Identifying specific learning characteris-

TABLE 6.1. LEARNING PROBLEMS AND COMPUTER-BASED EDUCATION

Learning Problems/ Characteristics	Special Category	Potential Computer Instruction Contribution		
		CBI	CMI	Compensatory Tool
Cognitive				
Poor organizational skills	LD, EH, MR, HR	X	X	
Attention deficits	LD, EH, MR, HR	X	X	X
Language-processing difficulty	SL, LD, MR, HR	X	X	X
Memory deficits	MR, HR, LD	X	X	X
Affective				
Low self-concept	All Categories	X	X	X
Low frustration level	EH, MR, HR	X	X	
Low motivation	HR, MH, ED	X	X	
Motor/Sensory/Physical				
Poor motor coordination	LD, MR, SL, PH		X	X
Visual-processing problem	LD, MR, VI	X	X	
Poor vision	VI	X	X	X
Poor hearing	HI	X	X	X
Physical disabilities	PH	X	X	X

EH = emotionally handicapped, HI = hearing impaired, HR = high risk, LD = learning disabled, MH = mentally handicapped, SL = speech and language disorder, PH = physically handicapped, VI = visually impaired

tics is sometimes straightforward, as in the case of hearing or visually impaired students. Identifying learning characteristics of individual students and making appropriate curricular modifications or adjustments, however, is not easy. As you have seen in Figure 6.1, learning problems may occur at any point during the learning process. Some students are poorly organized and lack cognitive strategies to assist with the semantic encoding process, the process of organizing and making sense out of newly perceived information for storage in long-term memory. Other students may have impaired sensory capacities of vision or hearing. Once a problem is identified, specific and sometimes extensive modifications are required in the instructional activities and procedures.

One of the main points made in chapter 3 is that instruction with a computer is only as effective as the instructional content delivered by the computer. A poorly designed instructional program will not be effective just because it is presented by a computer. When designing CBI, all the components that need to be considered in effective instructional design must be addressed and tailored to emphasize specific aspects of the instructional process in response to individual learning needs of students.

The remainder of this chapter will discuss instructional features to look for in computer-based instructional programs to facilitate the learning process of students with specific types of learning problems.

LEARNING CHARACTERISTICS AND COMPUTER-ASSISTED INSTRUCTION

Computer-based instruction offers teachers a unique opportunity for planning and presenting learning activities for the specific needs of special learners. Later we will discuss the specific features to look for when planning CBI for students with various types of learning problems. Each problem area will be discussed in terms of the recommended CBI instructional feature needed for appropriate modification of instruction.

Students with Learning Problems Related to Information Reception

As pointed out in Figure 6.1, all learning of new information begins with the reception of stimuli through the receptors, or the sensory modalities of vision, hearing, touch (tactile), and smell (olfactory). In formal learning situations, such as schools, the reception of new information usually occurs through vision or hearing. Most of us take our vision and hearing capabilities for granted. However, it is estimated that approximately one of every 1,000 school-age children is either blind or partially sighted, and one in 500 has a hearing loss great enough to be considered handicapped (Berdine & Blackhurst, 1986). For these students, the use of computers as a compensatory tool, as well as for instruction, has dramatic implications.

Visual Impairments. A blind or seriously visually impaired student is at a great disadvantage in a public school. Most teachers rely heavily on visual aids, including chalkboards, films, filmstrips, charts, and worksheets. Almost all homework assignments involve the use of textbooks and/or worksheets or other printed or graphic materials.

With the introduction of voice synthesis devices, computers can offer an excellent tool to compensate for the lack of vision. A voice or speech synthesizer can be attached to a computer to approximate the sound of a human voice. There are two main types of speech-generating computer technologies. Although both utilize a process of digitization of speech sounds, one approach uses a phoneme base and the other a whole word or phrase base. By far the most frequently used speech peripheral used in schools today is the phoneme-based speech synthesizer. This device converts text to speech by applying letter-to-sound rules that produce basic units of speech (phonemes). The synthesizer converts the phonetic units into sound waves that approximate human speech (Omotayo, 1983). The most popular phoneme-based speech synthesizers in schools today are the Echo II, Echo PC, and Cricket, all produced by Street Electronics in Carpinteria, California, and Votalker, produced by Votrax International in Troy, Michigan.

With the use of phoneme-generating speech synthesis, the intelligibility of the speech output is of primary importance. Phoneme transition, usage, combinations, and inflections are quite complex in normal speech and are difficult to duplicate (Bozeman, 1985). As a result, most of the phoneme-based synthesizers have a very mechanical, or robotic, quality to their output. A few studies have attempted to determine the ability of children to understand phoneme-based computer synthesized speech. It is not surprising that one study (Laddagga, Levine, & Suppes, 1977) found that word-based digitized speech (defined later) is easier for elementary students to understand than the phonemene-based, robotic-sounding speech. Rhyne (1982) found that the ability of blind children to comprehend a phoneme-based speech synthesizer incorporated in the Kurzwell Reading Machine improved as a result of practice. More recently, a study conducted with public school learning-disabled students found that, with practice, 67 percent of words presented with a phoneme-based speech synthesizer (Echo II) were correctly identified, as compared to 94 percent correctly identified from voice recordings of words (Helsel-Dewert & Vandenmeiracker, 1987). The Echo II study also indicated that intelligibility improves with practice.

The second type of speech synthesizer uses a waveform digitization technique that seeks to reproduce the speech sound exactly as it originally occurred. This procedure uses a voice input device, like a microphone, to "speak" words or phrases to the computer. The system records the voice sound through a waveform digitization process. This technology requires that all the digitized words be retained in memory, in contrast to the phoneme-generating type of synthesizer, which only needs to retain a complete set of phonemes (around sixty-four) in memory. The speech produced by the word-digitization process is of very high quality and sounds very much like the human voice. Studies on the intelligibility of high quality word digitization devices indicate word recognition rates of above 90 percent (Helsel-Dewert and Vandenmeiracker, 1987).

Although the digitized word-based speech synthesis technique is clearly much more satisfactory in terms of voice quality, until recently the memory requirements were too expensive to be practical. With the phoneme-based synthesizer, only the phoneme rules are retained in the program memory, and the computer can speak an infinite number of words with various phoneme combinations. In contrast, all words to be used in a word-based system have to be digitized, catalogued, and saved to memory. Hence, a large dictionary of words must be available for quick access in this type of synthesizer. There is a trade-off between speech quality and the size of the memory and processing overhead. At present, speech synthesizers with lower cost ($125 to $200) and poorer voice quality are being used much more frequently. With the increasing availability of low-cost, large-capacity memory chips, however, the digitized speech devices may become more practical. It is quite possible that the cost of the larger amounts of processing and storage memory will drop to the extent that the higher-quality, word-based synthesizer will become the synthesizer of choice in most educational settings.

As a result of the advances in speech synthesis technology, an increasing array of computer software is becoming available, designed to generate voice as well as screen information. See Box 6.1.

The emergence of voice capabilities through speech synthesis technology has opened up a number of practical uses for blind and severely visually impaired students. Several word-processing programs (such as Word Talk, Bank Street WriteR, and Text Talker) have been designed to be used with synthesizers. These programs allow the student not only to hear what she or he is typing but also to "listen" to any text file that is compatible with the word-processing program. Some programs, like Word Talk (Grim & Miller, 1985) are designed with blind students in mind. Auditory cues indicate the cursor's position on the screen in relationship to the text. Special functions keys turn off and on the various special features of the program.

Another emerging application is software that will direct the computer/speech synthesizer to "read" any text that is presented on the screen. These programs are developed to run simultaneously with other application programs. This type of generic speech synthesis software

---

Box 6.1   Instructional Features That Facilitate Learning of Visually Impaired Students

Use software/hardware that includes the following:

1. word-processing software with voice synthesis that reads letters, sentences, and screens
2. instructional software that is programmed to be used with a speech synthesizer
3. generic voice-activating software to use in tandem with any instructional software
4. large-type monitors and software for partially sighted students

program will enable blind students to use some of the popular instructional software programs that students with normal vision use extensively. Moreover, the blind student can independently move through the instructional material at his or her own rate. An example of this type of software program is the Verbal Operating System, produced by Computer Conversation, Columbus, Ohio. There is one major drawback in the widespread use of a generic voice-activating software system. Software that has certain types of "copy protect" systems may not operate interactively with voice-activating software. This presents the PC compatible users with less of a problem than Apple II series users because only a small percentage of PC compatible software is locked or copy protected. Even with this drawback, however, it is quite conceivable that in the near future a significant amount of a visually impaired student's instruction will be given by a computer with an attached speech synthesizer.

Hearing Impairments. A student who is deaf or has a severe hearing impairment presents a formidable task for teachers and schools. A hearing impairment has extensive implications for instruction and learning. The hearing loss will affect the student's receptive and expressive language abilities and, hence, his or her ability to communicate (Lindsey, 1987). Because of the heavy reliance on visual (screen displays) reception and tactile (keyboard entry) response, computer-based instruction can be used very effectively for individualizing instruction for deaf and hearing impaired students. Box 6.2 lists some of the important instructional software features that can be used to facilitate individual instruction of hearing impaired students.

Box 6.2 Instructional Features That Facilitate Learning of Deaf and Hearing Impaired Students

Use software/hardware that includes the following:

1. voice-recognition communication systems to translate speech into print
2. on-line help programs that provide the student with visual directions and assistance on request
3. visual menus, directions, and instructions to assist the student with use of the program
4. graphics, charts, outlines, and/or maps to assist the student with understanding and organization
5. specially designed language and vocabulary development programs for hearing impaired students

---

The availability of voice input systems provides the potential for vast improvements in the communication abilities of hearing impaired students. A voice recognition device (VRD) is a mechanism (hardware and software) that reliably transforms human or human-sounding speech into symbol strings that can be presented on the screen or sent to a printer. Using a microphone attached to the computer through a VRD connection, a teacher can "speak" to a deaf student. The spoken words are interpreted by the computer and immediately presented on the computer screen. Currently, most commercial VRDs limit the length of the speech utterance to under two seconds. Single words or short phrases are recognizable by these units, which are called isolated word VRDs.

Continuous word VRDs account for a much smaller percentage of use. This type of VRD permits the user to enter longer strings of words. although it has a sentence-length limitation to the speech input. One advantage is that continuous word VRDs enable the user to approximate natural speech more closely. Consequently, they are easier to use. A big disadvantage of the continuous word VRD, however, is the amount of processing power needed. The cost of the computer needed to interface with the continuous word VRD is much higher than the cost of a less powerful microcomputer needed to interface with an isolated word VRD. Nevertheless, the voice recognition devices hold a great deal of promise as a compensatory tool for hearing impaired students. Educators concerned with deaf students should be exploring the use of this technology for instruction. With the assistance of the latest technology many deaf students can be appropriately and optimally educated in regular schools and classrooms.

Another software feature that is very helpful to deaf and hearing impaired students is on-line help, which refers to the availability of additional directions, instruction, or explanations within the software program. Most on-line help information is accessible by using a special function key or control key. Usually the additional information relates to using the software program. Occasionally, help systems are used in CBI programs to provide additional tutorial or instructional information. Most help components are contextual. That is, the additional instructional information is related to the aspect of the program that the student is working on at the moment. Since students with severely impaired hearing learn primarily through sight, additional visual instructions keyed to the students' needs can be extremely helpful.

Using this same rationale, it is advisable to select software that provides frequent visual aids within the program. The assistance may be in the form of detailed, step-by-step directions, menus, pictures, charts, outlines, or maps that clarify and add to the understanding of the program content.

Students with Learning Problems Related to Information Processing

Many of the learning problems displayed by students with learning disabilities, mental retardation, and emotional and behavioral disorders, as well as students labeled high risk, are related to the sensory registor and memory phases of Gagne's information-processing model of learning. These basic cognitive processes involve focusing attention on appropriate information, organizing and coding information, and remembering information. To continue the analogy of computer functioning and human learning, the counterpart to attention, organizing, and remembering is the computer's information processing as regulated by the applications software and the processing memory (short-term memory). Floppy disks and/or hard disks are the components of the computer that reflect long-term memory storage.

Attention Problems. A number of children that have problems learning academic content appear to have difficulty focusing their attention on the learning task in any sustained manner. Many students diagnosed as learning disabled (though certainly not all) have difficulty attending to the learning task. As a result, a significant subgroup of learning-disabled students has been identified as having an "attention deficit disorder" (American Psychiatric Association, 1981).

Attention also seems to be related to the effective instruction literature as it applies to time on task. Whether students demonstrating inattentiveness to the learning task have a specific attention deficit or problems in other cognitive areas (such as problem-solving strategies or task organization) remains a debatable issue among experts (Mercer, 1987). Regardless of the learning theory construct from which the topic is approached, students demonstrating a lack of attention to the academic task present a major instructional problem for many teachers.

Although there have been few attempts at empirically documenting the effects of various computer applications of instruction with learning-disabled students, the studies that have been conducted are encouraging. In summarizing this research, Torgesen (1986) concludes that there is substantial evidence that computers can be programmed to deliver effective instruction in reading and math to learning-disabled students. What remains to be demonstrated, however, is the relative effectiveness of specific CBI procedures compared to already available, less expensive instructional procedures.

Lack of empirical evidence notwithstanding, a number of logical arguments have been advanced advocating the use of CBI to focus the learner's attention on the academic task, particularly if the academic task is of a drill and practice nature (Senf, 1983; Torgesen & Young, 1983). One of the earliest approaches to structuring academic instruction for children with attention problems advocates the enrichment of the instructional stimuli accompanied with a reduction of the noninstructional stimuli (Cruickshank, Bentzen, Ratzeburg, & Tannhauser, 1961). Examples of attempts at increasing the stimulus value of the instructional information are procedures using (1) multisensory (i.e., visual, auditory, tactile) instructional materials, (2) highlighted visual cues (words that are color-cued) and (3) study carrels to reduce the noninstructional stimuli.

Box 6.3 lists instructional features or events that can be used to facilitate attention on the learning task. Look for these features in software for students demonstrating a lack of attention and/or distractability.

By now it should be clear that there is no substitute for specific instructional objectives at the beginning of an instructional activity. Use of instructional objectives tells the student with poor attention the purpose of his or her attention-focusing efforts. The instructional objectives should be specific enough to communicate to the student what he or she needs to focus on and what accomplishments are expected. Although many instructional software programs specify objectives in the teacher's manual (or *documentation*), most of the kindergarten through grade twelve courseware available today does not begin a lesson with the objectives specified. If the courseware is addressing several objectives, it would be helpful to begin each subsection of the lesson with a specific

---

Box 6.3 Instructional Features That Facilitate Focusing Attention on the Learning Task

Use software/hardware that includes the following:

1. specific instructional objectives to tell the student what he or she is to focus on
2. attention-focusing features to highlight the essential instructional information on screen (large print, color, inverse highlight)
3. avoidance of software with special features that draw attention away from the relevant instructional content such as animation, sound effects, or high-resolution graphics
4. multiple sensory modalities (such as simultaneous use of screen text and voice synthesis)
5. limited amount of instructional information presented at any one time; content broken into logical chunks of specific information

objective. Another approach that has seldom been used is to keep the objective visible on each instructional screen addressing the objective—either at the top of the screen or boxed in the upper right-hand corner.

Although the study of attention deficits leaves a number of questions unanswered concerning the effectiveness of various compensatory instructional procedures, some educators have focused on distinguishing between the relevant instructional stimuli and the nonrelevant, or noninstructional, stimuli. From an instructional design viewpoint, there is a need to draw attention to the information to be learned and reduce the stimulus value of the surrounding noninstructional information. A number of the educational games now available on the market violate these design principles. Many educational game programs increase the stimulus value of the noninstructional information, using pictures (graphics) that promote the game aspects of the software but have no relationship to the instructional objectives or the content to be learned. Examples of this type of courseware include math drill games that display game-related graphics on the screen. If the student provides the correct response to the problem, a monster is destroyed, a plane is shot down, or man-eating tiger is dispatched. Although the graphics appear appealing and motivating, they draw attention away from the learning task. If a motivational reward for responding correctly to a problem is desired, the positive reinforcement should appear after the response on a separate screen from the instructional stimulus.

Methods of drawing attention to the relevant instructional stimuli include the use of large-print text, a distinguishing color, and at times highlighting of the text. Some courseware overuses color or highlighting to the extent that it is distracting in itself. Such software should be avoided.

As discussed earlier, the increasing amount of courseware that provides synthesized voice simultaneously with the text that appears on the screen can also be useful for students that have difficulty focusing their attention. For years special educators have used multisensory approaches to teaching language arts. This approach is based on the premise that some children learn best when content is presented in several modalities at the same time. These approaches have traditionally been referred to as the VAKT (visual-auditory-kinesth ic-tactile) approach. The Fernald method and the Gillingham method for teaching reading both feature a multisensory approach to instruction (Mercer & Mercer, 1985).

Recent studies on the attention problems of learning-handicapped students suggest that the critical attributes of the learning task are related to the cognitive complexity of the task (Krupski, 1985). These findings suggest that it is important to limit the amount and complexity of the instructional information presented at any one time. For example, instead of presenting a task with several logical steps as a total chunk of information on the screen at one time, it would be more appropriate to have each of the steps presented, responded to, and practiced separately—in sequence. After each separate aspect of the task is mastered, as demonstrated through the student's responses, the total integrated task should be presented and practiced.

Problems with Organization and Memory. Many low-achieving students appear to have difficulty organizing and remembering basic information essential for satisfactory academic achievement. As mentioned earlier, memory problems relate to the individual's ability to organize and attach meaning to new information in a manner that will facilitate long-term storage of the information. The ease of retrieval of that information, when needed, is also an important aspect of adequate memory capabilities.

A number of important instructional strategies can be incorporated in instructional software to facilitate and enhance the ability to remember academic information. Many of these instructional strategies will be familiar because they are related to the principles of effective instruction discussed in chapter 2 and the instructional design principles presented in chapter 3. Box 6.4 lists several important features to look for in selecting software for students that are having difficulty with organization and memory.

As discussed earlier, it is important to review previously learned

---

Box 6.4   Instructional Features That Facilitate Organization and Memory Abilities

Use software/hardware that includes the following:

1. begins the lesson with a review of related information previously learned to provide a framework for tying new information to information already in memory
2. outlines, maps, charts, or diagrams to show how new information relates to already learned information
3. uses meaningful graphics on screen to associate new information with known information
4. employs on-line review and rehearsal of metacognitive memory strategies (lists of definitions, rules, examples, mnemonics, keywords, or steps displayed on screen at all times or available through a special function key)

information that relates directly to the topic to be taught. This review helps the students bring to mind the information already learned that will be integrated with the information to be learned. The old information provides a structure, or foundation, to which the new information can be linked. Based on the same principles, use of outlines, charts, graphs, or diagrams can help the student fit new information into a framework that is already familiar to the student. Meaningful pictures or graphics also help tie new information to information already learned. For example, when teaching Celsius temperature measurements, a picture of a thermometer illustrating the freezing points for both the Celsius and Fahrenheit measurements will relate the known information (Fahrenheit freezing point) with unknown information (Celsius freezing point).

Related to the need to review previously learned information are strategies using outlines, charts, maps, and/or diagrams to show how new information relates to information that has already been learned. These visual aids help the students organize new information. Many students who have difficulty learning academic materials lack learning strategies used to organize new information. To assist these students, metacognitive learning strategies have been developed. Metacognition refers to knowledge about thinking. Able students appear to be more aware of their own cognitive processes and the procedures they use to learn new information (Wolfolk, 1987). For example, when students use such strategies as identifying the main idea, forming associations and images, creating mnemonics, rehearsing information, and outlining, they are monitoring their own learning processes.

Computer-based instruction is an ideal medium for building into the courseware design these types of learning strategies. To illustrate, a number of mnemonic devices have been developed that use the first letter of key words to remind the student to proceed through a series of steps. COPS is the mnemonic acronym for an approach developed at the University of Kansas (Deshler, Warner, Schumaker, & Alley, 1983) to assist students with written language development. In this acronym, C stands for capitalization, O for overall appearance (e.g., spacing, legibility, neatness), P for punctuation, and S for spelling. As students review a first draft of their written work, they use the mnemonic acronym to remember each step of the review (Alley & Deshler, 1979).

Courseware that has built-in automatic review devices can be very useful for students with memory difficulties. The TICCIT (Merrill, Schneider, & Fletcher, 1980) computer-based instructional system is an example of instructional software that can be developed with built-in organization and memory aid components. Intended for adult instruction, TICCIT has built-in subprograms that (1) allow the student to review the rules underlying the instructional content, (2) provide examples, and (3) provide practice of the rule or concept being taught (Alessi & Trollip, 1985). These aids are interactive with the content being taught, providing help at any point in the tutorial. As courseware becomes more functional, it is anticipated that built-in learning strategies will become more prevalent.

Students with Learning Problems Related to Language Expression

The final phases of the information-processing learning model, response generator and effectors, relate to the individual's ability to organize and express information in such a manner that demonstrates understanding of the information learned. Some students demonstrating academic difficulties have problems organizing their thoughts and expressing them— either verbally or in writing. Speaking and writing skills are essential for success in public schools. It is through these modes of expression that the student demonstrates his or her understanding of the information learned. Without these skills, students may know the content but have a difficult time demonstrating that knowledge.

Computer applications for students having expressive language difficulties can be divided into four basic categories. In addition to the three categories presented earlier in Figure 6.2—CBI, compensatory tools, and CMI—a third category, clinical treatment, will also be discussed briefly.

CBI. Computer-based instruction applications developed for the normal school population may be used very successfully with pupils that display expressive language problems. Most CBI tutorial programs do not require verbal or written expression to demonstrate mastery of the instructional material. Usually, responses are in the form of selecting the appropriate response from a set of multiple responses. Occasionally the response calls for filling in the blank with an appropriate word. Hence, there is very little reliance on verbal or written expression, allowing the student with an expression problem to demonstrate his or her cognitive abilities without penalty for the disability.

Compensatory Tool. If there were a vote taken on the most useful application of computers in today's society, word processing would no doubt win. As a compensatory tool for students with expressive language problems, particularly written language, word processing can be used very effectively. As is the case with most new instructional applications, the personal testimonials supporting the use of word processing far exceed the supporting empirical evidence available. Nevertheless, the testimonials of students with poor written expression are very impressive.

Actually, the question of general effectiveness of word processors is basically a moot point. The professions of law and business have not found it necessary to conduct empirically based studies to determine whether or not word processors increase work effectiveness. Almost all lawyers and businesspersons who can afford them, however, use word processors. Their observations have evidently convinced them that word processors save time and money.

To date, there have been very few studies reporting the effectiveness of the word processor to facilitate the written expression of students with various learning problems. The studies that have been conducted with handicapped and/or low-achieving pupils suggest that when a word processor is used to write letters or stories, (1) more time is devoted to the writing task, (2) more revisions are made, and (3) longer letters or stories are written. Also, students prefer a word processor over paper and pencil (Durham County Schools, 1986; Vacc, 1987). On the other hand, the studies have not found that the *quality* of writing (i.e., expression of ideas) has improved, even though the ease of reading the written document has improved.

In some schools, a debate has been triggered concerning whether or not low-achieving and handicapped students should be allowed to use word processors in demonstrating their written language skills. It is sometimes argued that if handicapped or disadvantaged students use word processors it gives them an unfair advantage over students who do not use word processors. It seems that this debate could be easily settled by a clear delineation of the instructional objectives. If the objectives are related to developing written communication skills that will facilitate the student's contribution to society, word processing should be quite acceptable. If, however, the instructional objective is much narrower and focuses on improving the student's handwritten communication skills, then indeed, a word processor would be out of bounds for obtaining that objective.

Frequently, students with poor written communication skills are also poor spellers. The use of spelling check programs can not only speed up the editing process but also remediate spelling weaknesses. Spelling check programs quickly compare each word in a document that the student has created with each word in a dictionary to see if there is a "match." When no matching word is found in the dictionary, it is assumed that either the word is misspelled or the word does not exist. Most spelling check programs allow the user to add words to the dictionary to accommodate unusual words that are used frequently, such as technical words or proper nouns. To help the student correct misspelled words, most spelling check programs will display a set of correctly spelled words that resembles the spelling of the incorrectly spelled word. Usually, the program will display one option. Sometimes, however, because the program does not know which word to select from several similar words, several options are displayed. Many students can select the correct spelling if they see the word spelled correctly. Spelling check programs provide not only a fast and accurate method for editing spelling—reducing the amount of time needed for editing—but also instructional experience. When a particular word is frequently misspelled and corrected several times, the student becomes familiar with the correct spelling. See Box 6.5 for a list of instructional applications for students with poor written communication abilities.

Augmented Communication. Use of computers to compensate for serious handicaps and disabilities is a very exciting and noteworthy effort in the application of computer technology to the needs of special populations. Although still in the development stage, a great deal of work has been done in applying computer technology to assist severely handicapped individuals with communication skills. With the legal mandates to provide instructional opportunities for handicapped pupils within the mainstream of regular education, all educators should be aware of the availability of computer-based adaptive devices that facilitate the communication process of severely handicapped students. These devices have been developed for individuals who do not have the physical capacity to operate a keyboard manually (input or receptors) and/or do not have understandable speech (output or effectors).

To assist handicapped students with access to computers, various forms of touch pads with large alphabet letters are used. Touch pads are

---

Box 6.5   Instructional Applications for Students with Poor Expressive Language Abilities

Use software/hardware that includes the following:

1. CBI tutorial programs for basic skills instruction
2. word-processing programs to facilitate writing and compensate for written language difficulties
3. spelling check programs to compensate for poor spelling ability and spelling remediation
4. use of augmentative communication devices for severely handicapped students
5. specialized clinical and remedial treatment programs designed for treatment of specific expressive language disabilities

basically substitute keyboards that provide a larger or more accessible "target" for the students' motor input. To facilitate communication, various overlays can be used with touch pads. For example, a touch pad and speech synthesizer can be used together to provide instruction to cerebral palsied, nonvocal, or other seriously impaired students. Pictures of objects can be taped to the touch pad representing vocabulary being taught. Upon request, the student selects the word by touching a picture. The increased pressure on the point of the touch pad activates the program to "speak" the name of the object. With these devices nonverbal, handicapped students can communicate with others by touching the symbol, words, objects, or letters. The system is programmed to respond through the speech synthesizer with a phrase, such as "I would like to go outside," or with letters and words—depending on the physical and/or mental abilities of the student. The Prentke Romick Company in Wooster, Ohio, specializes in computer hardware and software systems that facilitate the communication process of handicapped individuals. The programs Touch Talker and Light Talker have become an inseparable part of the daily lives of many quadriplegic and cerebral palsied students across the country.

Clinical Treatment. Computers have been found to be useful in the clinical treatment of individuals with speech and voice disorders. Peripheral instruments attached to a computer have been developed that can provide either visual and/or auditory feedback on parameters of speech such as frequency, intensity, nasalization, vocal onset, vocal harshness, and respiration patterns (Rushakoff & Bull, 1986). A device called the Visa-Pitch has been used successfully for the treatment of voice disorders. When attached to a computer with a voice input device, the Voice-Pitch system can produce both numeric and visual data that visually represent a speech pattern. This application provides the user with a visual display of his or her speech output. When used for clinical treatment, the student works on matching his or her visual speech pattern, as seen on the computer monitor, with a normal sample displayed on the computer monitor. Using this technique with a student with a bilateral hearing loss and voice/speech disorder, Rushakoff and Edwards (1982) reported positive results.

Gifted and Talented Students

Gifted and talented students are frequently identified in the public schools as students with special educational needs. They are defined as those students "identified by professionally qualified persons who, by virtue of outstanding abilities, are capable of high performance. These are children who require differentiated educational programs and service beyond those normally provided by the regular program in order to realize their contribution to self and society" (Kirk & Gallagher, 1986). Because of their potential and creativity, gifted or talented students are frequently provided with additional "enrichment" activities within the public school curricula. With the increasing availability of computers in the schools, these enrichment activities often involve computer applications. Speciality software programs for talented students include (1) creative writing, art, drawing, and music composition; (2) desk-top publishing; (3) project planning; and (4) computer programming.

Actually, these uses of computers should be viable applications available to all students. It is clear, however, that programs for the gifted and talented have been in the forefront in taking advantage of the variety of computer uses that can facilitate critical thinking, creativity, and productivity. Box 6.6 identifies three general topics that address the different applications available to all students for the development of critical thinking and creativity.

Computer Programming. Most educators assume that bright, advanced students should have the opportunity to learn more about computers as a topic of study. Hence, gifted and talented students are quickly introduced to the realm of computer science. For the most part this means learning how to control the computer through understanding and using programming languages. Several levels of programming tools are available— programming languages, authoring languages, and various levels of authoring systems. Currently, BASIC is probably most frequently used in public schools because it is readily available and is compatible with most computers. Other frequently used languages include PASCAL and C language. Although not considered a tool for serious programming by computer science specialists, LOGO is also frequently used to introduce

---

Box 6.6   Applications to Facilitate Development of Higher Order Computer Skills

Use software/hardware that includes the following:

1. programming languages including BASIC, PASCAL, and LOGO
2. authoring systems to develop instructional and other types of software
3. special use software tools for creative expression such as word processing, graphic arts, publishing, and music composition

students to programming. LOGO was originally introduced by Papert (1980) to be used not only as a computer language but also as a tool for developing problem-solving and critical thinking skills, abilities that many believe remain underdeveloped in most of our public school graduates. Initial studies however, have not been very encouraging (Pea & Kurland, 1984).

Authoring Computer Programs. Currently, there are three major categories of programming and/or authoring software tools that can be used to teach students how to create software. These tools vary in difficulty and in flexibility. The three main categories are programming languages, authoring languages, and authoring systems. Table 6.2 illustrates the relationships of the three types of authoring tools in terms of power, characteristics, and ease of use.

Programming Languages. Traditionally, software programs have been created (or authored) through general-purpose computer programming languages, such as FORTRAN or BASIC. Although BASIC is still the language most frequently taught in public schools, professional programmers are primarily using PASCAL and/or C languages (Hannum, 1986; Merrill, 1985). The main advantage of using a programming language for developing the code for software lies in its power and flexibility. Programming languages include a wider range of commands that take advantage of the logic capabilities of the computer. With a programming language, an author can create any type of software, with complex graphic displays as well as complex conditional branching. A section of a BASIC language code from an instructional program is shown in Figure 6.2. This set of coded instructions is converted to machine language and executed. In general, a programming language is much more economical in the amount of central processing memory and storage space needed. Even though many texts and short courses are available for learning how

TABLE 6.2. COMPARISON OF AUTHORING TOOLS

Type	Description
Programming language	A coding system that allows the creation of instructions that the computer understands
Authoring language	A coding system, specific to authoring, that is understood by a subprogram that executes the instructions
Authoring system	A software program that allows the user to select parameters for creating instructional lessons that are interpreted by a built-in coding system

```
100   REM AREA OF A TRIANGLE
110   PRINT "in the previous lesson you learned how to determine
120   PRINT "the area of various geometric figures. Let's review
130   PRINT "the formula for the area of a triangle."
140   PRINT
150   PRINT "A = 1/2*B*H
160   PRINT
170   PRINT "What does the 'B' in the formula stand for?"
180   INPUT ANS$
190   IF ANS$ = "BASE" GOTO 220
200   PRINT "No, that is not correct. Try again."
210   GOTO 180
220   PRINT "Correct, 'B' is for the base of the triangle."
230   PRINT
240   PRINT "Now, what does the 'H' stand for?"
250   INPUT ANS$
260   IF ANS$ = "HEIGHT" GOTO 290
270   PRINT "No, that is not correct. Try again."
280   GOTO 250
290   PRINT "Very good! Now try this problem"
300   PRINT "What is the area of a triangle with a base of 8
310   PRINT "and a height of 30?"
320   INPUT AN
330   IF AN = (8*30)/2 GOTO 360
340   PRINT "No, your answer is wrong. Try again."
350   GOTO 320
360   PRINT "Correct!"
```

Figure 6.2. A segment of BASIC language code. (SOURCE: Techniques for creating computer-based instructional text, by W. Hannum, 1986, *Educational Psychologist, 21,* (4), 293–314.) Reprinted with permision of Laurence Erlbaum Associates.

to use a general-purpose programming language, they are difficult to master (Hannum, 1986). Many individuals who have learned how to use a general programming language remain novices compared to a relatively few programming experts who command the programming language and logic to the extent that they can create almost any piece of software in a short time.

Authoring Languages. Authoring languages are computer programming languages that have been developed specifically for creating instructional software. Authoring languages are designed to interact with a programming language. The programming language interprets the authoring language code and executes it. A major advantage of an authoring language over a general-purpose programing language is the inclusion of special-purpose subroutines that address frequently used features. For example, frequently used features in most software include information

```
R:  AREA OF A TRIANGLE
T:  In the previous lesson you learned how to determine
 :  the area of various geometric figures. Let's review
 :  the formula for the area of a triangle

 :  A = 1/2*B*H

 :  What does the 'B' in the formula stand for?
A:
M:  base
TN: No, try again
NJ: @A
TY: Correct, B stands for base.
 T: What does the 'H' stand for?
A:
M:  height
TN: No, try again.
NJ: @A
TY: Very Good! Now try this problem.
 T: What is the area of a triangle with a height of 8
 :  and a base of 30?
A:
M:  120
TN: No, your answer is wrong. Try again.
NJ: @A
TY: Correct!
```

Figure 6.3. A segment of PILOT programming code. (SOURCE: Techniques for creating computer-based instructional text, by W. Hannum, 1986, *Educational Psychologist, 21,* (4), 293–314.) Reprinted with permision of Laurence Erlbaum Associates.

presentation screens (text, displays, graphics), user response inputs, and branching (often referred to as matching or linking) (Merrill, 1985).

Compared to programming languages, authoring languages are easy to learn and use. The commands used in developing authoring language codes are usually mnemonics for the task to be performed (Hannum, 1986). For example, a *T:* followed by text might indicate that this specific text is to appear on the screen at this time; or an *A:* might indicate a spot to accept a response from the pupil. A general purpose programming language might require several commands to accomplish the same task that takes only one or two commands with an authoring language. Commonly used authoring languages include Apple Computer's Super-PILOT (1982), EZ PILOT (Hartley Courseware, 1982), and MacPILOT (Micropi, 1985). An example of a segment of an instructional program written in PILOT (IBM, 1985) is illustrated in Figure 6.3. This segment of PILOT code accomplishes the same instruction as the segment of BASIC code illustrated in Figure 6.2.

Authoring Systems. An authoring system allows the user to create software without directly writing computer codes (Eisele, 1985; Hannum, 1986). The author can select various parameters from a series of menus to design screens, specify pupil-computer interactions, and determine screen relationships. An authoring system is a comprehensive computer program that translates the screen designs, pupil-computer interactions, and screen relationships into code the computer understands through an interpretation process. Kearsley (1982), in a slightly different definition, defines authoring systems as a comprehensive computer program that generates the computer code to present instructional lessons based on information supplied by the user. Authoring systems can be very simplistic and limited in terms of the type of instructional software that can be developed, or they can be very comprehensive, flexible, and sophisticated. Hannum (1986) divides authoring systems into three levels: first-level systems, second-level systems and third-level systems. The major feature of the highest level authorizing system is the flexibility in controlling the content of the software. Some of the more sophisticated systems allow the user to control the use of the software.

Special-Use Computer Applications. Several application tools are particularly useful for gifted and talented students, as they are for almost all students. A *word-processing* program frees the student from the fine motor mechanics of writing to allow concentration on the content and organization of what is being written. With many talented students, the development of ideas and thoughts occurs much faster than they can be written in longhand. A word processor (assuming the student has typing skills) encourages the student to write a first draft mainly to generate and capture the ideas and thoughts. The first draft can then be easily and quickly edited for punctuation, spelling, organization, and grammar. The major prerequisite for word processing is typing skill (a number of educators refer to typing skills taught with a word processor as "keyboarding skills"). To take advantage of the availability of computers and word-processing software, many schools are introducing typing at an earlier age.

Computer-based graphic art and drawing programs are also recommended for the development of creative skills. Several methods are available for using these types of programs, including graphic pads, light pens, and a mouse or joystick. Excellent examples of graphic art programs with an attached mouse (a device, familiar to most students, that controls the movement of the cursor on the screen) are MacPaint (used with the MacIntosh microcomputer) and Paintbrush (used with IBM PC compatible microcomputers). With the appropriate software, students can create graphic art; save the artwork to disk; and use it in newsletters and/or other publications.

The process of turning words and pictures into a good-looking newsletter, article, newspaper, or manual is a tricky business that calls for a combination of various artistic and writing talents, as well as the appropriate computer software. *Desktop publishing* is a growing and popular application that can facilitate the creative abilities of talented students. New software combined with laser printing make it possible for one or two persons to control almost all aspects of the publishing process. Traditional school activities involving a school newspaper, parent newsletters, or the annual yearbook are now being turned out using desktop publishing software. With such software programs as PageMaker (Aldus Corporation, 1987) and Ventura Publishing (Xerox Corporation, 1986) high-quality publications can be developed. Comprehensive use of these programs will take some detailed instruction, but then motivated and talented students can independently plan and develop a variety of creative publications.

Another application to explore is the array of new *music composition* programs available. These programs not only introduce the novice musician to the world of music but can also be a very helpful tool for the accomplished musician. Technological advances have improved the sound capabilities of computers through music synthesizers. Examples of programs available to use with the Apple II microcomputer are Electronic Art's (1983) Music Construction Set and Mindscape's Bank Street MusicR (Clancy, 1984).

SUMMARY

There is a trend in public schools to focus on group instruction to facilitate mastery of basic education skills in language arts and mathematics; at the same time there is also a larger range of individual differences in the typical classroom. Almost every public school class today has one or more mainstreamed exceptional students enrolled, as well as a continuum from poorly motivated and low-performing students to highly motivated and high-performing students. In this chapter we have suggested that how students learn is similar to how computers process information. We have presented an information-processing learning model as a basis for making decisions in the selection of computer application programs and activities to facilitate the instruction of students with various types of learning problems.

With the availability of voice input and speech synthesis devices, computers can be used to compensate for vision and hearing disabilities. Likewise word-processing applications can be employed to compensate for learning problems and disabilities at both ends of the information-processing sequence—receiving information and expressing information. Many learning problems are associated with difficulties in focusing attention, organizing and storing information in memory, and organizing and retrieving information from memory. The design of courseware can be extremely important in facilitating the learning of students who have poor processing abilities. Poor design of courseware can exacerbate learning problems and contribute to ineffective instruction.

Finally, we have presented brief discussions on the use of computers for compensating for the serious disabilities of multiply handicapped students and for the involvement of creative, motivated students in the development of higher-order computer skills associated with the design and production of software and courseware.

PUTTING THE BOOK TO WORK

Read each question, review the relevant section of the chapter, and write a response.

Question	*Source*
1. Why is it important that all teachers have knowledge and skills in using computers with students with special learning problems?	122
2. How does the learning process compare with how computers process information?	123
3. What are the phases and functions within an information-processing model of learning?	123–125
4. What are some specific computer application features that can be used to facilitate the instruction and learning of (a) blind and/or visually impaired students, and (b) deaf and hearing impaired students?	128–132
5. What are some examples of computer application features that can be used to facilitate the focusing of attention on the learning task?	133–135
6. What are some examples of computer application features that can be used to facilitate organization and memory abilities?	136–137
7. What are some examples of computer application features that can be effectively used with students demonstrating poor expressive language abilities?	138–141

8. What are some examples of computer applications   141–147
that can facilitate development of creative,
higher-order computer skills?

9. What are the similarities and differences among   143–146
programming languages, authoring languages, and
authoring systems?

CHAPTER 7

Courseware Evaluation

Objectives

After reading this chapter, you should be able to do the following:

1. Define *content validity* and describe how it operates in the evaluation of instructional software (courseware).
2. Cite and describe the three main areas addressed in evaluating courseware.
3. Cite and describe the criteria for rating the instructional content of courseware.
4. Cite and describe the criteria for rating the instructional procedures found in a courseware program.
5. Cite and describe the criteria for rating the instructional management features of courseware.

INTRODUCTION: THE WHY AND HOW OF COURSEWARE EVALUATION

Many educators contend that one of the biggest obstacles to comprehensive use of computers for instruction is the lack of effective and efficient courseware. The instructional courseware available, in general, does not receive high marks. A major goal of commercial software publishers is to produce software that will sell. Unfortunately, software features that are perceived to increase sales usually are not the same features that are identified as conveying the principles of effective instruction and instructional design.

Numerous articles have been written on how to evaluate courseware, usually accompanied with a suggested approach for conducting software evaluations. In this chapter we will construct a framework for approaching the task of evaluation of courseware and provide procedures to facilitate the evaluation task. In doing so, much of what we have presented in the previous sections of this book will be synthesized and applied to the courseware evaluation process. The Longman Courseware Checklist, developed by the authors, will be presented as a suggested approach for the evaluation of instructional software.

The ultimate purpose of the evaluation of instructional software is to determine its level of validity. Although the concept of validity is used primarily in the field of tests and measurements, it is also applied effectively to the evaluation of instructional materials. Validity refers to the degree to which a test, or in this case, an instructional software program does what it is supposed to do. If a courseware program is supposed to teach third-grade students to recognize the main idea in a written paragraph, to what extent does it meet this goal?

Several types of validity may be established for courseware, including predictive validity, content validity, and construct validity. The predictive validity of a courseware program addresses the extent to which the use of the courseware produces the predicted results. The only way an evaluation of the predictive validity of courseware can be conducted is through the experimental research design utilizing the courseware in question. An approach frequently used to evaluate the predictive validity of a courseware program involves establishing experimental and comparison groups of students. The experimental groups use the courseware being evaluated, and the comparison groups use non-CBI approaches to instruction on the same academic topic. As any educational researcher will tell you, there are a lot of pitfalls involved in this approach. It is very difficult to control the many variables that may have an impact on the outcome of the study in addition to the experimental variable—the CBI courseware. Therefore, it is quite difficult to design a study that will allow you to say with confidence that the resulting gains in achievement are due only to the experimental variable, in this case a specific piece of instructional courseware. Even if it were easier to design and implement a sound experimental study, the time it would take to conduct such a study for each new courseware program would make this approach very time consuming. Nevertheless, it is often argued that it is the responsibility of the commercial courseware vendor to field-test and "validate" all courseware programs offered for sale to schools. In fact, however, this does not happen. Nor does it happen with other commercially available instructional materials, such as basal textbook series or supplemental instructional programs.

Another, more frequently used approach to the evaluation of courseware is one that involves the concept of content validity. In the context of courseware evaluation, content validity refers to the extent that the content of the courseware is able to produce the intended instructional results. If the content and the instructional procedures presented in the courseware are judged to be representative of what is known (through documented educational research) about effective instruction of a specific skill, content validity is obtained. The courseware evaluation procedures presented in this chapter use a content validity approach to determining the extent that the courseware represents what is known about the specific instructional content, instructional design, and instructional effectiveness. By now you should be quite familiar with this content, as it was presented in detail in the previous chapters.

EVALUATION PROCEDURES

A comprehensive evaluation of computer courseware should include a review of three main aspects: (1) instructional content, (2) instructional procedures, and (3) instructional management. *Instructional content* refers to the subject of the instruction. For example the courseware may be designed to teach capitalization skills, verb usage, or identification of nouns. To evaluate the appropriateness of the courseware it is important that the content is presented accurately and clearly, with the proper emphasis on the main points or principles to be learned. In addition, the evaluation of the content should include a review of how appropriately the content is organized to promote learning, taking into account the effective instructional practices discussed in some detail in chapter 2.

Evaluation of the *instructional procedures* incorporated into the courseware is based on the accepted and proven principles of instructional design. This aspect of the courseware evaluation responds to the general question of how the courseware is designed to optimize learning within a CBI format and is based on the principles presented in chapter 3 on instructional design.

Finally, the evaluation should take into account the instructional management features of the courseware. As discussed in chapter 4 *instructional management* refers to the process of keeping track of the progress of each individual student using the courseware. Instructional management is not only important for providing timely feedback to the student on his or her performance but also extremely important in the development of lesson plans and progress reports to parents.

USING THE LONGMAN COURSEWARE
EVALUATION CHECKLIST

To assist educators with the task of conducting an informed evaluation of instructional software, the Longman Courseware Evaluation Checklist has been developed and is presented in the following pages. The checklist (see pages 171–172) incorporates what is known about effective instruction and the design of effective instructional materials. Twenty criterion items are presented across the three areas of instructional content, instructional procedures, and instructional management.

To conduct an evaluation with the Longman Courseware Evaluation Checklist, thoroughly review the discussion on each item and then review the courseware that is being evaluated. If at all possible, observe students using the courseware from beginning to end. Each item on the checklist is rated on a five-point scale, with five designating the highest rating. A rating of five indicates that you strongly agree with the statement in reference to the courseware that is being evaluated. A rating of one is the lowest rating that can be given and indicates that you strongly disagree with the criterion statement. A brief description of each of the twenty items follows.

Instructional Content

1. Objectives Are Clearly Specified. The instructional objectives for the courseware lesson(s) should be presented at the beginning of the program so that the student working on the lesson knows what it is that she or he is trying to accomplish. This practice is clearly supported in both the effective instruction research and in accepted instructional design principles. Clearly specifying the objectives provides the student with specific learning expectations (Winne & Marx, 1982), directions, (Good & Brophy, 1984), and the basis for evaluation of mastery of the objective (Bloom, 1976). Paradoxically, an examination of currently available courseware indicates that the specification of objectives at the beginning of a lesson rarely occurs. A few programs clearly specify the objectives of the courseware in accompanying teacher's manuals, which is certainly helpful. However, objectives should be communicated clearly to the learner as the first step of the instructional process. Figure 7.1 provides a simple illustration of how an objective can be presented at the beginning of a courseware lesson.

2. Intended Audience Is Clearly Identified. The need to specify the intended audience for the courseware is closely related to specifying the instructional objectives clearly. A first step in developing any instructional lesson involves specifying the characteristics of the students that

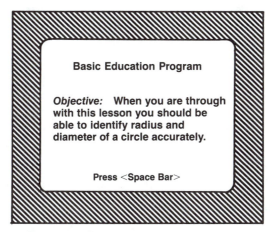

Figure 7.1. Objectives are clearly specified.

will be receiving the lesson. Was the courseware developed for advanced students or primarily as a remedial lesson? At approximately what grade level is the lesson intended to be used? Was the lesson developed for a population of children that have special learning characteristics, such as slow learning, disabled learning, or language and communication problems? Upon a review of instructional software catalogues of the major publishers and distributors of courseware, it is clear that many publishers do not like to be specific in identifying intended audiences. As a result you will frequently see a large range listed as appropriate for the courseware. One catalog reviewed indicates grade spans of 3–12, K–6, 8–12, 4–8, and 2–12 for specific courseware programs. Can the same courseware program be used appropriately across five or six grade levels? On the other hand, some publishers go to great lengths to give as much detail about the intended audiences as possible. Hartley Courseware in Dimondale, Michigan, uses seven categories to indicate the intended audience (pre K, 2–3, 4–6, 7–9, 10+, adult literacy, GED prep., and special needs). Some publishers, however, confuse the reviewer by indicating that courseware can be used across several categories or levels. See Figure 7.2 for a sample catalog page of Hartley Courseware.

3. Content Appropriately Reflects Objectives. A careful review of the courseware should allow you to determine the extent to which the content covers the information suggested in the objectives. If the courseware has clearly stated its instructional objectives, this task should be relatively easy for most educators. However, if there are no objectives or the objectives are stated in very vague terms, it will be difficult to give the courseware a high rating on this criterion.

CHECKLIST OF FEATURES

PROGRAMS	Page No.	Color Graphics	Large Letter Set	Sequenced Frames & Questions	Information + Random Questions	Hints or Explanations Used	Multi-Level Lessons	Branch If Too Easy or Difficult	Missed Items Repeated	All Content Is Modifiable	Some Content is Modifiable	Individual Recordkeeping	Records May Be Printed	Class Summaries Available	Pre/Post Tests Available
		GRAPH		INSTRUCTIONAL DESIGN						TEACHER CONTROL AND MANAGEMENT					
VOCABULARY: RECOGNITION AND MEANING															
Vocabulary – Dolch	27		●				●	●		●		●	●	●	
Vocabulary – Elementary	27		●				●	●		●		●	●	●	
Vocabulary – Controlled	27		●				●	●		●		●	●	●	
Vocabulary Create	27		●				●	●		●		●	●	●	
Word Families	28		●		●		●	●		●		●	●	●	
Word Families II	28		●		●		●	●		●		●	●	●	
Student Word Study	28								●		●	●	●		
Opposites	29		●		●	●	●	●	●	●		●	●	●	●
Memory Match	29	●			●		●		●	●		●	●	●	●
Wordplay	30	●	●		●		●			●		●	●	●	
Word Ladders	30	●			●		●			●		●	●	●	
Word-A-Tach															
Analogies Tutorial	31		●	●		●	●	●	●	●		●	●	●	●
Analogies Advanced	31			●		●	●	●	●	●		●	●	●	●
Analogies College Bound	31			●		●	●	●	●	●		●	●	●	●
WORD ANALYSIS															
Vowels, Consonants	32		●	●			●	●		●		●	●	●	
Vowels Tutorial	32		●	●			●			●		●	●		
LITERARY SKILLS															
Figurative Language	33			●		●	●	●	●	●		●	●	●	
Intellectual Pursuits	33				●							●	●		
Shakespeare	33				●							●	●		
Harper and Sellers	34														

Figure 7.2. A sample publisher's catalog checklist specifying the characteristics of courseware. (Reprinted with permission from Hartley Courseware, Inc., Dimondale, MI, Fall, 1987.)

156

CHECKLIST OF FEATURES

PROGRAMS	Page No.	EQUIPMENT REQUIRED						TARGET GRADE LEVEL							PROGRAM TYPE			
		Apple II+, IIe, IIc, IIGS	IBM, PC, Tandy 1000, MS-DOS	Cassette Control Device	Printer	Echo or Cricket	64K Apple or 256K MS-DOS	Pre-K to 1	2–3	4–6	7–9	10+	Adult Literacy, GED Prep.	Special Needs	Instruction & Practice	Drill	Game & Strategy Building	Tool or Authoring
VOCABULARY: RECOGNITION AND MEANING																		
Vocabulary – Dolch	27	●		●				●	●				●	●		●		
Vocabulary – Elementary	27	●		●				●	●				●	●		●		
Vocabulary – Controlled	27	●		●				●	●				●	●		●		
Vocabulary Create	27	●		●				●	●	●			●	●		●		
Word Families	28	●	●					●	●				●	●		●		
Word Familiies II	28	●							●				●	●		●		
Student Word Study	28	●								●			●				●	●
Opposites	29	●	●										●	●		●		
Memory Match	29	●	●						●	●			●	●			●	
Wordplay	30	●								●							●	
Word Ladders	30	●								●							●	
Word-A-Tach																		
Analogies Tutorial	31	●	●							●			●	●	●			
Analogies Advanced	31	●	●								●		●		●			
Analogies College Bound	31	●	●									●	●		●			
WORD ANALYSIS																		
Vowels, Consanants	32	●		●				●	●				●	●			●	
Vowels Tutorial	32	●		●					●				●	●	●	●		
LITERARY SKILLS																		
Figurative Language	33	●	●								●		●		●			
Intellectual Pursuits	33	●	●											●			●	●
Shakespeare	33	●	●											●			●	●
Harper and Sellers	34	●												●				

Figure 7.2. (Continued)

4. Introduction Provides Clear Directions. As we discussed in chapter 2, the nature of the learning task should be clearly and concisely explained to the student. Most courseware will have two types of directions: (1) directions for manipulating the computer, and (2) directions for interacting with the content presented. Directions for manipulating the computer (e.g., SELECT A NUMBER AND PRESS RETURN) should always appear in the same spot on the screen—usually at the bottom. In some programs, when the task is similar from screen to screen, the directions are gradually phased out, the assumption being that the student understands the routine. The examples in Figure 7.3 show the initial instructions given on Screen A. On the next screen (Screen B), the program assumes that the student understands that she or he is to type in the letter designating the response choice. More explicit directions on Screen B would be: TYPE THE LETTER INDICATING YOUR SELECTION. PRESS <RETURN> FOR A HINT.

5. Lesson(s) Begin with a Review of the Relevant Content. Educational research has demonstrated that students achieve more when lessons begin with an initial review of previously learned information relevant to the present task (Emmer, Sanford, Clements, & Martin, 1982; Kozma, 1982). Beginning a lesson with a review of prerequisite information helps the learner recall and review information and skills that are pertinent to the present learning. Unfortunately, very few courseware programs begin their instruction with a review of the major prerequisites for the lesson. An example of a review screen is presented in Figure 2.2.

6. Content Is Presented Fluently, Precisely, and Clearly. Students learn more when difficult words and long phrases are avoided, when transitions are made smoothly, and when a lesson continues to move forward at an even pace (Hiller et al., 1969; Smith & Cotton, 1980; Smith & Edmonds, 1978). Good courseware programs are designed so that the information presented is precise and nonrepetitious, unless the repetition is desirable for learning. Ambiguous terms should be avoided, and the content should be presented with precision. Usually, the content of most courseware has been well planned and will earn a high rating on this criterion. Sometimes, however, attempts at increasing motivation, such as elaborate game-oriented graphics, will add extraneous and irrelevant information.

7. Content Is Challenging but Allows for High Rate of Success. Educational research has found that high-success activities are associated with higher levels of student on-task behavior, higher achievement, and more appropriate student social behavior (Emmer, et al., 1982; Fisher et al., 1978; Kozma, 1982). Well-designed courseware will provide conditional

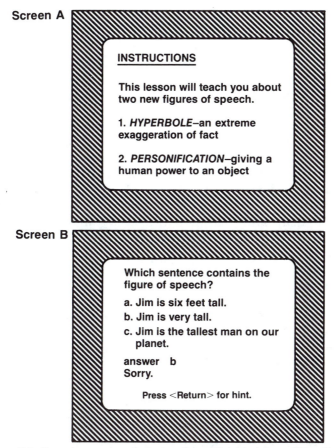

Figure 7.3. Sample courseware instructions. (Adapted from *Figurative Language*. Reprinted with permission from Hartley Courseware, Inc., Dimondale, MI.)

branching based on the student's responses, which will minimize low rates of success. If a student begins to have difficulty with the content, the program should quickly take the student back to an easier, prerequisite level. Once the easier material is mastered, the program brings the student back to the more challenging content better prepared to interact favorably with the program.

8. Content Is Broken into Reasonable Chunks of Information. The text of the courseware should be carefully organized into logical parts, components, or "chunks" of information. Frequently, the courseware content is organized around rules or principles. One chunk of information might include a concise presentation of the rule followed by several applied examples. Other, related screens might provide practice tutorial activities. When reviewing courseware for this criterion, rate as low programs that present several screens of information without reviewing or outlining the content or interjecting an interactive response from the student. See Figures 7.4 and 7.5 for examples of "nonchunked" and "chunked" screens.

9. Concepts and Language Are Appropriate for Intended Audience. The clarity with which lessons are presented is directly related to student on-task behavior. The match between the vocabulary and examples presented in the courseware and the vocabulary level and experiences of the students using the program is very important (Cooley & Leinhardt, 1978; Emmer et al., 1981). This criterion may be difficult to apply unless you have actually observed the behavior of various students as they are using the courseware.

10. Main points and/or Principles are Frequently Reviewed or Summarized. As discussed in chapter 2, research findings have been consistent in reporting a relationship between reviewing or summarizing and student achievement (Armento, 1976; Emmer et al., 1982). Every CBI lesson should contain summaries of the material covered. Not only are summaries or reviews at the end of a lesson important, but also brief subsection

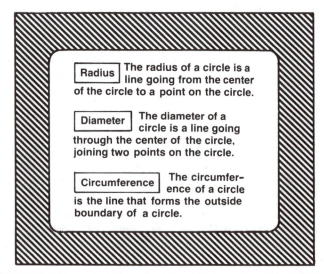

Figure 7.4. Example of nonchunking of information on a screen

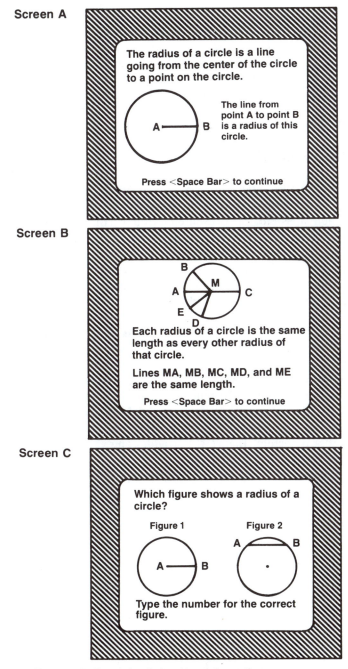

Screen A

The radius of a circle is a line going from the center of the circle to a point on the circle.

The line from point A to point B is a radius of this circle.

A———B

Press <Space Bar> to continue

Screen B

Each radius of a circle is the same length as every other radius of that circle.

Lines MA, MB, MC, MD, and ME are the same length.

Press <Space Bar> to continue

Screen C

Which figure shows a radius of a circle?

Figure 1

Figure 2

A———B

Type the number for the correct figure.

Figure 7.5. Example of chunking information on screens

summaries of the main points or rules covered in a section of the lesson are helpful. The most common form of summaries and/or reviews are quizzes and posttests covering the instructional information presented in the lesson. Unless immediate corrective feedback is given, however, a test may not be the best method of summarizing the material. Clear, concise summaries of the main rules, points, or principles presented in the lesson are found infrequently, particularly in commercial courseware. Figure 7.6 shows typical review screens.

Instructional Procedures

11. Content Is Presented through a Variety of Procedures, such as Examples, Illustrations, Analogies, Flowcharts, and Outlines. Content should, when possible, be presented through concrete examples, analogies, metaphors, illustrations, outlines, and flowcharts (Carter, 1985). These various modes of presenting content help the student fit new information into a framework of information that is already familiar. Courseware using a variety of these instructional presentations relevant to the content should be rated highly on this criterion (see Figure 7.7).

12. Frequent Interactions Are Spaced Throughout the Lesson(s). The primary advantage of CBI is its interactive capabilities. Except for a one-to-one tutorial session with a teacher, the interactive capability of CBI is hard to match with other available instructional approaches. Unless this feature is used frequently through interactions and tutorial feedback, its advantage may be lost. Tutorial, or corrective, feedback to the student requires more than just an indication of whether the response was correct or incorrect. Figure 7.8 provides an example of an interactive sequence of two screens. When an incorrect response is made, feedback should be given about why the response was incorrect as well as additional information to assist with selecting an appropriate response.

13. Instructional Feedback Is Clear, Concise, and Avoids Superficial Motivators (e.g., GREAT! GOOD JOB!). Feedback should be brief, clear, and to the point. The best feedback for correct responses is simple and concise, such as THAT'S RIGHT or CORRECT. Students are not motivated by exaggerated feedback, such as WOW! PERFECT! FANTASTIC! TERRIFIC! In fact, some students feel that the program is trying to manipulate them with hyperbole and are turned off by such exaggerations.

14. Instructional Feedback After Incorrect Responses Is Specific and Shows Why the Response Is Incorrect. Unless the courseware is strictly drill and practice, feedback upon incorrect responses should provide

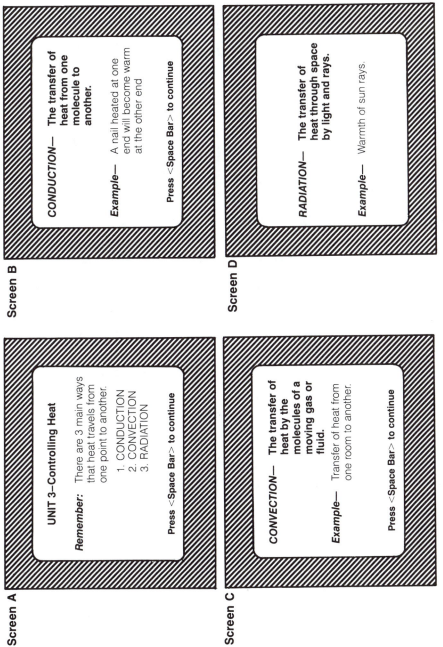

Screen A

UNIT 3—Controlling Heat

Remember: There are 3 main ways that heat travels from one point to another.

    1. CONDUCTION
    2. CONVECTION
    3. RADIATION

Press <Space Bar> to continue

Screen B

CONDUCTION— **The transfer of heat from one molecule to another.**

Example— A nail heated at one end will become warm at the other end

Press <Space Bar> to continue

Screen C

CONVECTION— **The transfer of heat by the molecules of a moving gas or fluid.**

Example— Transfer of heat from one room to another.

Press <Space Bar> to continue

Screen D

RADIATION— **The transfer of heat through space by light and rays.**

Example— Warmth of sun rays.

Figure 7.6. Summary of main points in a lesson

163

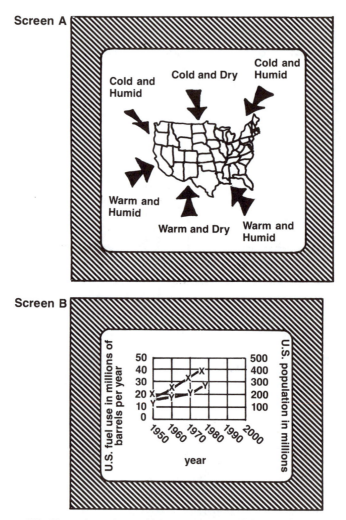

Figure 7.7. Examples of graphics on screen. (Adapted from *Holt Earth Science,* 1978. Published by Holt, Rinehart & Winston.)

corrective tutorial information. Courseware that does not do so is not using the full capabilities of the CBI. A sample corrective tutorial feedback screen is displayed in Figure 7.8.

15. Rate of the Presentation of Information Is Controlled by the User. At the simplest level, if a program advances only when the student responds, either by pressing RETURN, pressing the space bar, or making

Screen A

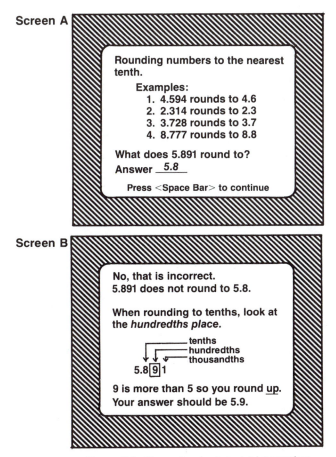

Rounding numbers to the nearest tenth.

Examples:
1. 4.594 rounds to 4.6
2. 2.314 rounds to 2.3
3. 3.728 rounds to 3.7
4. 8.777 rounds to 8.8

What does 5.891 round to?

Answer ___5.8___

Press <Space Bar> to continue

Screen B

No, that is incorrect.
5.891 does not round to 5.8.

When rounding to tenths, look at the *hundredths place.*

tenths
hundredths
thousandths
5.8⬚9⬚1

9 is more than 5 so you round up.
Your answer should be 5.9.

Figure 7.8. Example of a tutorial interaction

an entry, the rate of presentation is under the control of the student. At a more sophisticated level, however, additional control devices are made available to the student. Some programs provide learning guidance that is controlled by the student. Learning guidance devices include the availability of help screens, rule screens, or even example screens that provide additional information about the concept or instructional information being presented. These additional aids are made available by pressing a specified control key. Thus, the use of these features is under the control of the student. A few sophisticated courseware programs allow the student to select different aspects of the tutorial, bypassing sections of the program that have already been mastered. Figure 7.9 illustrates learner control.

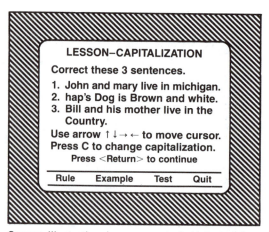

Figure 7.9. Screen illustrating learner control. (Adapted from *Temperature Experiments.* Reprinted by permission of Hartley Courseware, Inc., Dimondale, MI.)

16. Screens Are Designed to Draw Attention Only to the Relevant Information. Screens in an instructional courseware program should not be thought of as a printed page. The amount of text on the screen should be limited (Cohen, 1983). There should be a liberal use of white space, areas free of graphics and text. Screen layouts should be consistent throughout the program. Type face, margins, and the location of directions should remain the same across screens. Instructional screens in a CBI program should contain only that information that is essential to mastery of the objective (Jonassen, 1982; 1985). Frequently, software designers try to place too much information on one screen. Busy screens are more difficult to read, and it is more difficult for the student to concentrate on specific aspects of the information presented. Graphics and animation employed by many of the instructional game courseware programs can actually distract the student's attention from the relevant instructional stimuli. Screen A in Figure 7.10 should receive a high mark on this criterion. Screen B, on the other hand, illustrates a screen that would fail this criterion.

17. Text Sizes and Colors Are Appropriate and Do Not Draw Attention Away from Content. Larger text is appropriately used in many courseware screens. The text is easier to read, particularly for younger students. Sometimes a larger text or a different color will call attention to a key principle or rule within the text. If used judiciously, large text and/or a different color can, indeed, emphasize a specific word or phrase. However, frequent size or color changes can distract from the message

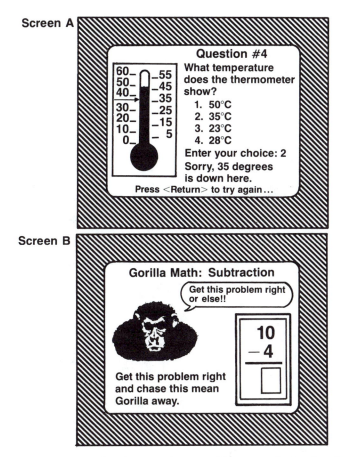

Figure 7.10A. Example of appropriate graphics on an instructional screen. (SOURCE: *Temperature Experiments.* Reprinted with permission from Hartley Courseware Inc., Dimondale, MI.) **B.** Example of inappropriate graphics on an instructional screen.

and should be avoided. When changing text sizes and changing colors distract from the instructional content, the program should be marked down on this criterion. Figure 7.11 illustrates a screen where different-sized text is used appropriately and a screen where different-sized text is used inappropriately.

Instructional Management

18. Courseware Provides Frequent Performance Checking and/or Testing. High-quality courseware will frequently measure the student's performance in relationship to the objective(s) for the lesson. The need

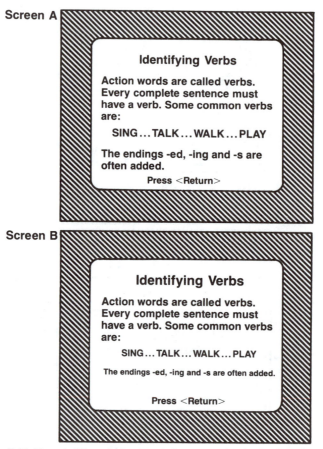

Screen A

Identifying Verbs

Action words are called verbs.
Every complete sentence must
have a verb. Some common verbs
are:

SING...TALK...WALK...PLAY

The endings -ed, -ing and -s are
often added.

Press <Return>

Screen B

Identifying Verbs

Action words are called verbs.
Every complete sentence must
have a verb. Some common verbs
are:

SING...TALK...WALK...PLAY

The endings -ed, -ing and -s are often added.

Press <Return>

Figure 7.11 Use of different-sized text: **A.** appropriately sized. **B.** inappropriately sized. (Adapted from *Verbs.* Reprinted with permission from Hartley Courseware, Inc. Dimondale, MI.)

for continuous monitoring and feedback on performance is consistently found to be an important practice in effective instruction (Good & Brophy, 1984; Stallings, 1978). The courseware available varies in the extent to which it meets this criterion. Sometimes the program will provide a cumulative count of how many responses during an interactive tutorial were correct and how many were wrong. This feature is helpful, particularly if the summary is aimed at the student and is easy to view and review. In addition, some courseware provides short mastery criterion tests before and after the lesson. This type of performance feedback can be extremely helpful, both to the student and to the teacher.

19. Keeps Continuous Records of Student Achievement. Comprehensive courseware that students use over a period of time covering a number of instructional objectives should keep a continuous record of each student's progress on objective mastery. This record is very helpful to the teacher in planning for individual instructional time as well as for subsequent instructional activities. The use of continuous record keeping is discussed in more detail in chapter 4.

20. Provides Clear, Concise Reports on Student Achievement and Summary Reports of Progress Across Students. This information is very helpful to teachers in planning for continuing instruction for each student. In addition it will provide feedback on instructional effectiveness across students that can be used for improvement of instructional techniques or the evaluation of the effectiveness of the courseware. Individual progress reports can be used very effectively in reports to parents.

VALIDITY AND RELIABILITY OF THE LONGMAN CHECKLIST

The Longman Courseware Evaluation Checklist is a criterion-oriented checklist developed to gather descriptive information on the quality of instructional courseware. Before any type of measurement device is used, it should be demonstrated that the device is valid and reliable. Within this context, *validity* refers to the extent that the checklist measures what it has been developed to measure—the effectiveness of instructional courseware. It is our task as developers of the checklist to build a case for the validity of the checklist. The content in each of the twenty items on the checklist has been extracted from what is known about effective instruction and what is known about effective instructional design. In chapters 2 and 3 we reviewed and discussed each of these bodies of knowledge—as gleaned from results of educational research on these topics. Thus, the content validity of the checklist is based on the extensive evidence available suggesting that the twenty items in the checklist reflect the criteria that the literature indicates are important as demonstrated through research.

The reliability of the Longman checklist can be calculated by computing the percentage of agreement between pairs of raters concerning the same courseware. To illustrate this procedure, two of the authors conducted a pilot reliability study of the checklist. The two raters spent one hour together reviewing each of the twenty criteria on the checklist followed by independent reviews of two separate courseware programs. The two independent ratings for each courseware program are presented in Table 7.1 along with the difference (D) score. As can be seen, the percentage of agreement across items was quite high. The lowest percentage of agreement between raters was found across the items rating instructional management. All other agreement percentages within the three subcategories were very high.

Based on the results of the procedures that we used to validate the content and to determine the reliability of the checklist ratings, we believe that this instrument can be used with confidence and that it will provide evaluative information about specific courseware programs.

TABLE 7.1. SAMPLE INTERRATER AGREEMENTS FOR EACH ITEM ON THE LONGMAN COURSEWARE CHECKLIST

	Ratings					
	Courseware 1			Courseware 2		
	R1	R2	D	R1	R2	D
Instructional Content						
1. Objectives specified	3	2	1	3	2	1
2. Intended audience identified	5	2	3	1	1	0
3. Content reflects objectives	3	2	0	3	2	0
4. Clear directions	2	2	0	3	3	0
5. Lesson(s) begin with review	1	1	0	1	1	0
6. Content presentation	2	2	0	2	2	0
7. Content challenging w/success	3	3	0	3	3	0
8. Content/information chunked	4	4	0	3	3	0
9. Appropriate for intended audience	3	4	1	2	3	1
10. Main points/principles summarized	2	1	1	2	2	0
Percent agreement (within 1 rating)			90%			100%
Instructional Procedures						
11. Variety of content presentation	2	2	0	2	2	0
12. Frequent interactions	4	4	0	2	2	0
13. Instructional feedback	1	2	1	2	2	0
14. Corrective feedback	1	1	0	2	1	1
15. User control	4	2	2	2	2	0
16. Screen designs	2	1	1	3	3	0
17. Use of text sizes and colors	4	3	1	2	3	1
Percent agreement (within 1 rating)			86%			100%
Instructional Management						
18. Student response records	4	1	3	2	2	0
19. Frequent performance checking	1	1	0	1	1	0
20. Student achievement status	1	1	0	3	2	1
Percent agreement (within 1 rating)			67%			100%
Total percent agreement (within 1 rating)			85%			100%

LONGMAN COURSEWARE EVALUATION CHECKLIST

COURSEWARE NAME: _____
PUBLISHER/DATE: _____
SUBJECT/LEVEL: _____

Evaluation Areas	Excellent		Poor
Instructional content	5	3	1
Instructional procedures	5	3	1
Instructional management	5	3	1

Criteria	Strongly Agree				Strongly Disagree
Instructional Content					
1. Objectives are clearly specified.	5	4	3	2	1
2. Intended audience is clearly identified.	5	4	3	2	1
3. Content appropriately reflects objectives.	5	4	3	2	1
4. Introduction provides clear directions.	5	4	3	2	1
5. Lesson(s) begin with a review of the relevant content.	5	4	3	2	1
6. Content is presented fluently, precisely, and clearly.	5	4	3	2	1
7. Content is challenging but allows for a high rate of success.	5	4	3	2	1
8. Content is broken into reasonable chunks of information.	5	4	3	2	1
9. Concepts and language are appropriate for intended audience.	5	4	3	2	1
10. Main points and/or principles are frequently reviewed or summarized.	5	4	3	2	1
Instructional Procedures					
11. Content is presented through a variety of procedures, such as examples, illustrations, analogies, flowcharts, outlines.	5	4	3	2	1
12. Frequent interactions are spaced throughout the lesson(s).	5	4	3	2	1
13. Instructional feedback is clear, concise, and avoids superficial motivators (e.g., GREAT! GOOD JOB!).	5	4	3	2	1
14. Instructional feedback after incorrect responses is specific and shows why the response is incorrect.	5	4	3	2	1
15. Rate of the presentation of information is controlled by the user.	5	4	3	2	1
16. Screens are designed to draw attention *only* to the information to be learned.	5	4	3	2	1
17. The text sizes and colors are appropriate and do not draw attention away from content.	5	4	3	2	1

Instructional Management

18. Provides frequent performance checking and/or testing.	5	4	3	2	1
19. Keeps continuous records of student achievement.	5	4	3	2	1
20. Provides clear, concise reports on student achievement.	5	4	3	2	1

SUMMARY: PUTTING THE BOOK TO WORK

To summarize the content of this chapter, make a copy of the courseware evaluation check list and select an instructional software program to evaluate. Thoroughly review the discussion in this chapter on each item in the checklist and then rate the courseware on each item. If you still have questions about specific checklist items, reread the appropriate sections of chapters 2 and 3. After the evaluation has been completed, respond to each of the following questions.

Question	*Source*
1. When rating courseware with the checklist, which items were the most difficult to rate? Why were those particular items difficult to rate?	154–169
2. When rating courseware with the checklist, which items were the easiest to rate? Why were these particular items easy to rate?	154–169
3. How did the authors determine the content validity of the evaluation checklist? Does this procedure seem to be reasonable for establishing the validity of the checklist? Why?	169
4. How did the authors determine the reliability of the checklist? Does this procedure seem to be reasonable? Why?	169–170
5. What is the most appropriate procedure to determine the effectiveness of instructional courseware? Why isn't that procedure used more frequently?	151–153

CHAPTER 8

Computers and Instruction in the Schools of Tomorrow

Objectives

After reading this chapter, you should be able to do the following:

1. Cite and describe four chronological phases of educational computing.
2. Cite and describe the three possible "futures" scenarios for the use of computers for instruction in public schools.
3. Cite and describe four potential changes in public school instruction stimulated by computer technology.
4. Describe the purpose of this text, as summarized by the authors.

INTRODUCTION: OPTIONS FOR THE FUTURE

Will computer technology lead American education into a new era of instruction and learning? The technology to support an affirmative answer to this question is certainly available. However, changing the patterns and practices established through the years in elementary and secondary public education in the United States presents an extraordinary challenge. As history has demonstrated, change in public education practice rarely takes place in any planned and timely manner. Unless there is a radical transformation in the process of change, the public schools in the United States may waste decades catching up with private enterprise in this country as well as more enterprising schools in other countries. The extent to which computers and computer-based instruction will be integrated into the mainstream of American education in tomorrow's schools will depend on the flexibility and acceptance of many different groups of people—teachers, teacher trainers, school administrators, parents, and policy makers. It will not be easy for computer technology to live up to its potential and become a tool for shaping significant new approaches to instruction.

Some educators predict that in ten or fifteen years you will be able to open the door of most school storerooms and find a pile of computers gathering dust in the dark—along with old filmstrip projectors. This prediction may prove to be not accurate, but there is no doubt that there will be a wide variation in the extent of, and in the type of, computer use in the schools of the future.

The extent of the application of computers in instruction will be quite different from state to state, school system to school system, and even from school to school within the same system. As Seymour Papert, professor of mathematics and education at MIT and author of the best-selling book, *Mindstorms* (1980), suggests, different schools will be using computers in different ways. His major fear is that computers will be used to centralize the control of learning (other educators hope that this development might be possible). Patrick Suppes, frequently identified as the father of computer-assisted instruction in the United States, predicts that the day will come when schools will use computers as they now use textbooks (Taylor, 1980). That is, they will be used extensively both in teacher-directed instruction and by students without supervision as a means for self-directed learning.

Is it only a matter of time before the use of computers is totally infused into the educational system? Bramble, Mason, and Berg (1985) suggest that we are now in the third of four evolving phases of educational computing. The first phase, the *experimental phase,* began in the early 1960s with a number of universities exploring the potential of computer-assisted instruction, using large, costly mainframe computers. The *popularization* phase began in the late 1970s, when the first generation of commercially produced microcomputers found their way into public school classrooms. The third phase, or *transition phase,* began in the mid-1980s, as the use of computers in schools increased dramatically and more and better courseware became available. It is suggested that the transition phase will continue to about the turn of the century, when the final phase, *infusion,* will begin. During the infusion phase computers will have an impact on all aspects of American education and will become an integral part of educational procedures. It is predicted that the continuing technological advances in computer hardware and software will have an important influence on the content and methods of education, and technological awareness will be crucial for the average citizen.

We will bring this book to a close with a discussion of three future possibilities: (1) Instructional procedures will continue as usual with the interesting and helpful addition of computer technology, (2) the use of computers in schools today is a passing fad and eventually will be abandoned, and (3) computer technology will provide the foundation and catalyst for major changes in how instruction and learning take place in the public schools.

SCENARIO I: INSTRUCTION AS USUAL WITH THE MISCELLANEOUS USE OF COMPUTERS

As discussed in chapter 1, currently there is widespread use of computers in the schools and there is some evidence suggesting that this use has a positive effect on the efficiency of instruction. Schools have found computers helpful as an additional instructional tool, to be used as one among many approaches. If current trends continue, computers will be used primarily for written communication and as a supplemental learning tool. These uses include (1) word processing as a tool for written communication, (2) computer literacy and computer science education to prepare for the use of computers in the world of work, (3) drill and practice and tutorial instruction, and (4) an entertaining reward—for getting assignments done on time or for good behavior in school.

At the present rate of the integration of computers into the schools, a small number of students in a few innovative schools will benefit extensively from computer-based learning tools and systems. However, students in the vast majority of schools will remain unaffected and will be technologically uneducated. Alfred Bork (1982), professor of computer science at the University of California at Irvine, predicts a rather gloomy future for the use of computers in schools. He suggests that there will be little progress made in the improvement of instructional software, and at the same time, schools will continue to deteriorate. Ineffective and unimaginative use of computers will contribute to this deterioration. One current and widespread practice that Bork strongly disagrees with is the use of computers for game playing as a reward for good behavior.

As the current practices continue into the future, relatively few schools will go beyond the use of computers in a supplementary role. Comprehensive computer-based integrated learning systems (providing diagnostic testing, tutoring, simulated learning scenarios, and continuous record keeping and progress reporting) will continue to be the exception rather than the rule. The basic design of the educational delivery system will remain unchanged, but computer technology will help facilitate the traditional approach to education and instruction in some schools.

SCENARIO II: THE DECLINE AND FALL OF COMPUTER TECHNOLOGY IN THE SCHOOLS

This scenario can be kept short—and gloomy. For the next five to ten years the use of computers will be very trendy, and all schools will provide some computer-based instruction to demonstrate that they are up to date and progressive. Teachers will continue to be exposed to many hours of in-service training on such topics as the bit and bytes of computers, computer literacy, word processing, and evaluating courseware. Eventually, however, the interest in computers across the curriculum will wane and basically disappear. As has been the case with slide projectors, film projectors, tape recorders, overhead projectors, and to some extent television, computers will be used more extensively at other levels of training, such as business and technical training. In the schools, however, the daily pressures and demands faced by teachers will preempt attempts to use computers in any comprehensive and significant manner. As a result, instead of additional and more creative use of computers in classrooms, less and less attention will be given to these machines.

A few schools and teachers will continue using computer-assisted instruction. These uses will focus on basic skills training to meet the increasing demands by states and legislators to focus on basic skills. The use of computer-based instructional management will continue to grow in special educational programs to facilitate individual instructional planning and progress monitoring. Some schools will continue to provide computer laboratories, primarily for the purpose of word processing. All in all, however, the romance between schools and computers will dwindle, and it will be education as usual, basically without computers.

SCENARIO III: NEW HORIZONS IN AMERICAN EDUCATION ON THE WINGS OF COMPUTER TECHNOLOGY

A number of experts predict that the increasing availability of computer technology will dramatically change the basic process of education as we know it today in our public schools. Instruction will be completely reorganized to take advantage of the ability of computers and computer-related technology to individualize and personalize instruction (Bramble, Mason, & Berg, 1985; Toffler, 1980). There will be an array of creative uses of computers in schools, motivated in part by a continuing public demand to improve the effectiveness of schools and in part by the creative integration of what is known about effective instruction and computer technology. A number of forces will come together to produce a techno-logical revolution in public education. Table 8.1 presents several of the major factors that will be involved and the resulting change in instruction. These factors include (1) public pressure to focus on accountability and instruction in the basic skills; (2) advances in computer technology that will provide large amounts of information storage, faster processing, and low-cost networking; (3) development of new and comprehensive courseware that will include voice input and output technology; and (4) development of comprehensive, integrated learning systems that will combine the best practices in instruction with the advances in computer technology.

TABLE 8.1. CHANGES IN PUBLIC SCHOOL INSTRUCTION STIMULATED BY COMPUTER TECHNOLOGY

Stimulant	Impact on Instruction
Public policy focus on acountibility and evaluation	Testing, test scoring, student progress monitoring, and system-wide analysis of student achievement will be conducted totally with the aid of computers, providing large savings in teacher time and costs.
Advances in computer technology	Large instructional information bases will become available at the building and classroom level, providing direct instruction, simulations, and comprehensive references.
Advances in computer software	Instruction will become highly individualized, using instructional systems with voice input/output that will diagnose, instruct, simulate, and monitor progress of students.
Integration of informed instructional practice and computer technology	CBI will become more efficient and time saving, demonstrating that basic skills in particular, can be developed through computer instruction and transferred to a variety of applications.

Public Policy, Accountability, and the Comprehensive Use of Computers

A trend already underway suggests that public school curricular scope and sequence is too important to be left to educators alone. National and state legislative actions relating to accountability, student evaluation, and testing will shape curricula as well as instructional procedures at the local level. In many states today, legislative mandates have established state-wide testing programs to monitor public school effectiveness. Testing programs will, in effect, establish the goals and curricular priorities of the public schools. To promote the implementation of their mandated educational programs, federal and state governments will encourage and support computer-based courseware production by establishing multi-million dollar development projects to produce comprehensive computer-based learning systems. Programs will be designed to collect data on the academic status and progress of individuals and groups of students across school systems. These efforts will be based on the advances in cognitive psychology and computer science providing intelligent instructional systems that can test, prescribe, teach, and retest students, measuring their progress and objective mastery with a high level of accuracy.

The cost of developing complex computer-based curriculum and information is, and will continue to be, high. Hence, the national and various state governments will be underwriting much of the cost—and will also control the decisions concerning the nature and content of the instruction. A side effect of these efforts, if not an intended outcome, is that public school curricula will become more standardized and the administration of education more centralized. Unfortunately, the influence that the typical classroom teacher will have on determining the content of what is taught in his or her class will be reduced.

Advanced Networking Technology

There are many reasons to believe that we will see an expansion of *computer networks* within school buildings and across school systems. There are several levels and types of computer networks, which include (1) local area networks (frequently referred to as LANS in computer science circles), (2) telephone modem networks, and (3) satellite networks. All three of these levels allow electronic communication among computers or computer terminals connected to the network. School buildings will primarily utilize local area networks, connecting a number of microcomputers or computer terminals by cables to the same hard disk file server or mainframe computer. Telephone modem networks are used when greater distances are involved, such as a network that links all the computers in several school buildings in a school system together and/or to a large hard disk file server located in a central office. Telephone modem networks actually can be used across any distance that is served by telephone. Satellite network systems use satellite communication to transfer computer software programs and information files from one location to another. The Maryland State Department of Education has recently installed a computer satellite network that will allow all the school systems in the state access to a central library of courseware and computer software. The courseware is "downloaded" from the satellite system into a central file server at the local education agency level. From that location, the courseware can be sent to any computer in the school system that is connected to the system-wide network.

Another, very obvious use of networking will be to provide rural and remote areas within states and regions access to current instructional information and courseware. This can be accomplished by operating a network in a similar fashion to the Maryland network. Not only can various educational agencies carry on two-way computer-based communications, but also schools and homes can be linked together for some exciting possibilities. The student who frequently leaves at school his or her homework assignment can sit down at a computer at home and request another copy. The assignment is electronically transferred from the school building's computer network to the home computer, and a hard copy can be printed (a side benefit will be better-organized homework). Taking the home-school computer network scenario a step further, the home will become an extension of the school, the home-school computer network being used for tutorials, assignments, and even testing and upgrading of objective mastery.

Many benefits accrue from networking. Instead of having the students and teachers at each computer station handle and load courseware, networks allow software programs and courseware to be selected from a table of contents that appears when a student signs on to the computer. Students and teachers never need to handle software. As the use of networks becomes more popular, every classroom, as well as offices in the school building, will have one or more microcomputers and/or computer-terminals. Students and teachers in each classroom can quickly and easily interact with the hard disk or mainframe system, either to load a courseware program into the memory of the classroom computer and run it, or to begin a continuous interaction with the mainframe computer. Courseware revisions and up-dates will also become much easier with the use of networks.

Currently, the use of networks is growing slowly in the schools, primarily because of the larger hardware costs associated with establishing extensive computer networks. The advantages of establishing wide networks will become more obvious as the costs decrease with advances in the technology. These advantages include the lower per pupil costs for courseware, the ease of manipulating courseware, and the interactive advantages provided by networks that are not available to isolated microcomputers. Certainly, the ease of using an array of various courseware programs will contribute to the increase in the popularity of network systems. Teachers and students can access the courseware much as they use an index in a book—by simply indicating on a menu screen which courseware they want to use.

Network systems will allow interactions between courseware programs and management programs that will streamline instructional planning and monitoring. When Jonathan Simpson turns on the computer and responds to a request to type in his name, the computer will take him directly to a courseware program that has been prescribed for him, based on a series of criterion referenced tests that he had previously taken on the computer. As Jonathan interacts with his various tutorial programs, the system will keep track of his performance and frequently inject mastery testing to update his performance record. Based on the results of his performance testing, new or additional tutorial programs residing in the system will be administered, resulting in a continuous cycle of testing and tutoring. These types of comprehensive, integrated learning systems, discussed in more detail in chapter 4, are available today. With these changes in the delivery of instruction, the classroom teacher's role will also change. When the objectives of the instruction are related to Bloom's (1971) categories of the development of knowledge, comprehension of knowledge, and the application of knowledge (see chap. 1), the teacher's role will be that of an administrator and manager of classroom instruction. However, when instructional outcomes are related to Bloom's categories of analysis, synthesis, and evaluation, the teacher's role will be to follow up the CBI with instruction aimed at facilitating the development of critical thinking, through such methods as Socratic dialogue.

Improvements in Instructional Courseware

As higher-quality and more sophisticated computer hardware becomes available, new, comprehensive courseware will be developed, particularly in the basic skills. To date, most instructional software is developed in the form of a single application—designed to teach a particular skill or ability. Teachers have to determine not only whether or not the courseware is any good but also when and how to use the program and where and how to store it. The difficulty of managing access to, and the storage of, seventy or eighty software packages circulating around an elementary school has been one of the factors contributing to the ineffective use of microcomputers in the schools (Bramble, Mason, & Berg, 1985). Software access and storage presents problems regardless of whether a school has established a computer laboratory or has individual computers located in various classrooms in the building. One solution to these problems involves the use of networks. Another involves the development and use of large, comprehensive CBI systems.

In chapter 5 we discussed artificial intelligence and expert systems in relationship to computer-based testing and student assessment. New courseware will allow the exploration of the feasibility of artificial intelligence for direct instruction. However, most of the new, improved courseware developed in the next decade will be only tangentially related to actual artificial intelligence. Highly effective courseware will rely heavily on sophisticated systems of instructional information (data) banks and IF-THEN logic programs. Information on call, or available to be used in tandem with courseware programs, will include comprehensive sets of instructional objectives; short tutorial programs correlated with each instructional objective; content information across all topics addressed by the courseware, similar to an electronic encyclopedia; simulated application problems; and corresponding mastery tests. With the emerging voice input and output (speech synthesis) technology, new courseware features will simulate human interaction to the extent that the software will interact with any type of response made by the student—a word, a phrase, or a complete paragraph. The following dialogue is an example of how a student will interact with an instructional courseware system sometime in the future:

STUDENT: [Turns on the computer]

COMPUTER: Hello, what is your name and today's date?

STUDENT: Jan Wilson, January 12, 1988

COMPUTER: Hello, Jan; the last time you worked on computer instruction was last Tues, January 5, 1988. At that time you spent 30 minutes working on Unit 10 in Earth Science, The Solar System: The Structure of the Sun. Would you like to continue that tutorial?

STUDENT: I would like to take a unit test to see if I have to study the sun any more.

COMPUTER: Which of the following mastery tests for The Solar System would you like to take?
1. The Structure of the Sun
2. Energy from the Sun
3. The Solar System
4. Mercury, Venus, and Mars
5. The Rest of the Solar System

STUDENT: 1.

COMPUTER: [At this point the computer administers a 30-item test measuring the objective of the first unit.]

COMPUTER: The results of your test indicate that you have mastered the following objectives:
1. Is able to compare the photosphere, chromosphere, and corona of the sun.
2. Is able to define *Sunspot,* providing an accurate description.
3. Is able to determine the rate at which the sun rotates with the use of sunspots.
However, you were unable to demonstrate mastery of the following objective (s):
1. Is able to explain accurately how the sun causes auroras on the earth.
Would you like to take a short tutorial on auroras?

STUDENT: Yes.

COMPUTER: *[Tutorial screen 1]* Auroras are caused by the sun. Do you have any idea what an aurora is?

STUDENT: I think it's a bright light in the sky at night.

COMPUTER: That's right. Do you know where the bright light is located?

STUDENT: Somewhere in the sky.

COMPUTER: That's true, but I was looking for a more specific answer. In what part(s) of the world would you look for an aurora?

STUDENT: I don't know.

COMPUTER: [Presenting a graphic showing solar particles being attracted to the north and south poles by the earth's magnetic field] Auroras (ah-roar-ahs) are caused by invisible particles, shot out of the sun, hitting the earth.

[Screen 2] [Continuing with the graphic] The earth's magnetic field causes these particles to be guided toward the north and south poles.

[Screen 3] [The same graphic is shown with additional illustration of the illuminated aurora] When the particles strike the gases in the earth's atmosphere, light is given off.

The aurora borealis is the aurora that is frequently seen in the northern hemisphere over the north pole. It is also referred to as the *northern lights.*

The computer-student instruction interaction can go on continuously, with a great deal of control of the direction given to the learner. The new generation of instructional courseware will incorporate many of the important principles of instructional design and what we know about effective instruction into the courseware—resulting in much more efficient learning, both in ability to transfer skills developed through computer interactions and in long-term memory of content information.

Teacher Authoring

Although there are some good reasons why it may not be desirable, or cost effective, to have teachers involved in courseware development, advances in authoring systems will make teacher authoring a real possibility. Just as in the past teachers have been extensively involved in developing their own teacher-made materials, the future will see many more teachers involved in developing their own courseware for their own classrooms. The main advantage of teacher authoring is the ability to address the needs of specific groups of students at the local level. Another, psychological advantage is the increased motivation of teachers when using instructional material they have designed and produced themselves. Sophisticated authoring systems, as we discussed in chapter 6, are becoming more available and, more important, are designed so that they will be very easy to use by nonprogrammers.

A serious difficulty with the first generation of courseware now being used in the public schools is that much of it has not been designed by professional educators and does not reflect an informed approach to instructional design. The major principle that has driven much of the courseware development to date is "Will it sell?" Thus, we end up with a lot of game-oriented courseware with graphics that not only are irrelevant to the objectives of the instruction but also actually work against them. Educators have perpetuated this practice by buying courseware that appears to be attractive and motivational, without concern that essential elements of effective instruction may have been eliminated. With classroom teachers becoming more involved in the development of their own courseware, they will become more aware of the deficiencies in other courseware that they may be using or reviewing. This does not mean that large numbers of teachers will become authors of commercial instructional software. The development of commercial courseware is very time consuming and expensive. However, teachers will become better selectors and users of commercial courseware as a result of using authoring systems to develop their own teacher-made courseware.

EPILOGUE: INTEGRATION OF INFORMED INSTRUCTIONAL PRACTICE AND COMPUTER TECHNOLOGY

It may be asking too much of the education profession to do a better job incorporating instructional design principles and effective instructional practices for instruction with computers than they have done with textbooks and other instructional materials. However, if computer technology is going to have a significant impact on public school education, the standards for courseware design and the implementation of computers in classrooms must be set very high. The purpose of this text has been to develop a bridge between what we know about effective instructional procedures and the use of computers for instruction in the public schools. Educational research has given the profession of education a solid foundation of information about effective instructional procedures and the effective design of instructional materials. This rich reservoir of knowledge cannot be ignored as we apply computers to the task of instruction. If it is, the high expectations that many have placed on the role of computers in the future of education will not be fulfilled. The extent to which we will see "education as usual" or dramatic and exciting changes in instruction stimulated by the wise and informed use of computer technology depends on teachers, school administrators, teacher trainers, and educational policy makers—that is, the education profession itself.

References

Aaron, I. E., Jackson, D., Riggs, C., Smith, R. G., Tierney, R. J., & Koke, R. (1981). *Scott, Foresman basic reading*. Glenview, IL: Scott, Foresman.

Aldus Corporation (1987). *Pagemaker* [Computer Program]. Seattle, WA: Author.

Alessi, S. M., & Trollip, S. R. (1985). *Computer-based instruction: Methods and development*. Englewood Cliffs, NJ: Prentice-Hall.

Alley, G., & Deshler, D. (1979). *Teaching the learning disabled adolescent: Strategies and methods*. Denver: Love.

American Psychiatric Association (1981). *Diagnostic and statistical manual of mental disorders* (3rd ed.) Washington, DC: Author.

Anderson, L. M., Evertson, C. M., & Brophy, J. E. (1979). An experimental study of effective teaching in first grade reading groups. *The Elementary School Journal, 79*(4), 193–223.

Anderson, L. M., Evertson, C. M., & Emmer, E. T. (1980). Dimensions in classroom management derived from recent research. *Journal of Curriculum studies, 12*, 343–356.

Anderson, T. H., & Armbruster, B. B. (1985). Study strategies and their implications for textbook design. In T. M. Duffy, & R. Waller (Eds.), *Designing Usable Texts*. New York: Academic Press.

Andrews, D. H., & Goodson, L. A. (1980). A comparative analysis of models of instructional design. *Jounral of Instructional Development, 3*(4), 2–16.

Apple Computer, Inc. (1982). *Apple Super PILOT* [Computer Program]. Cupertino, CA: Author.

Arlin, M. (1979). Teacher transitions can disrupt time flow in classrooms. *American Educational Research Journal, 16*, 42–56.

Armento, B. J. (1976, April). Teacher behaviors related to student achievement on a social science concept test. Paper presented at the annual meeting of the American Educational Research Association, San Francisco. (ERIC Document Reproduction Service No. ED 126 145)

Askeland, P. (1985). In D. Craighead (Ed.), *Microcomputers in education conference: Tomorrow's technology.* Arizona State University: Computer Science Press.

Ausubel, D. P., Novak, J. D., & Hanesian, H. (1978). *Educational psychology: A cognitive view* (2nd ed.). Englewood Cliffs, NJ: Educational Technology Publications.

Baker, F. B. (1978). *Computer managed instruction: Theory and practice.* Englewood Cliffs, NJ: Educational Technology.

Becker, J. H. (1987). Using computers for instruction. *Byte, 12* (2).

Becker, W. C. (1977). Teaching reading and language to the disadvantaged—what we have learned from the field research. *Harvard Educational Review, 47,* 518–543.

Becker, W. C., & Gersten, R. (1982). A follow-up of follow-through: The latter effects of the direct instructional model on children in 5th and 6th grades. *American Educational Research Journal, 19,* 75–92.

Berdine, W. H., & Blackhurst, A. E. (1986). *An introduction to special education* (2nd. ed.). Boston: Little-Brown.

Block, J. H. (1971). *Mastery learning theory and practice.* New York: Holt, Rinehart & Winston.

Block, J. H. (1972). Student learning: The setting of mastery performance standards. *Educational Horizons, 50,* 193–191.

Block, J. H., & Anderson, L. W. (1975). *Mastery learning in classroom instruction.* New York: Macmillan.

Bloom, B. (1971). Learning for mastery. In B. Bloom, J. Hasings, & G. Madaus (Eds.), *Handbook of formative and summative evaluation of student learning.* New York: McGraw-Hill.

Bloom, B. S. (1974). Time and learning. *American Psychologist, 682–688.*

Bloom, B. S. (1976). *Human characteristics and school learning.* New York: McGraw-Hill.

Borg, W. R., & Ascione, F. R. (1982). Classroom management in elementary mainstreaming classrooms. *Journal of Educational Psychology, 74,* 85–95.

Bork, A. (1982). Educational technology and the future. *Journal of Educational Technology Systems, 10*(1), 3–20.

Bozeman, W. C. (1985). *Computers and computing in education: An introduction.* Scottsdale, AZ: Gorsuch Scarisbrick.

Bramble, W. J., Mason, E. J., & Berg, P. (1985). *Comptuers in schools.* New York: McGraw-Hill.

Brown, J., & Burton, R. (1978). Diagnostic models for procedural bugs in basic mathematical skills. *Computer Science, 2,* 155–192.

Carnegie Forum on Education and the Economy (1986). *A nation prepared: Teachers for the 21st centry. The report of the Task Force on Teaching as a profession.* Washington, DC: Author.

Carnegie Foundation (1984). *A nation at risk: The report on the public schools.* Washington, DC: Author.

Carroll, J. B. (1963). A model of school learning. *Teacher College Record, 64,* 723–733.

Carter, J. F. (1985). Considerations in the development of distance education texts. In D. H. Jonassen (Ed.), *The technology of text: Principles for structuring, designing, and displaying text* (2nd ed.). Englewood Cliffs, NJ: Educational Technology Publications.

CBT/McGraw-Hill. (1984). *Microcomputer instructional management system* [Computer Program]. New York: Author.

CBT/McGraw-Hill. (1985). California Achievement Test. Monterey, CA: Author.

Center for Social Organization of Schools. (1985). *National survey on use of computers in education.* Baltimore: Johns Hopkins University.

Chambers, J. A., & Sprecher, J. W. (1983). *Computer assisted instruction: Its use in the classroom.* Englewood Cliffs, NJ: Prentice-Hall.

Chandler, T.(1982). Mastery learning: Pros and cons. *NASSP Bulletin, 66,* 9–15.

Chariot Software Group. (1986). *MicroGrade* [Computer Program]. San Diego, CA: Author.

Clancy, G. (1984). *Bank Street Music WriteR* [Computer Program]. Northbrook, IL: Mindscape, Inc.

Clark, R. E. (1986). Evidence for confounding in computer-based instruction studies: Analyzing the meta-analysis. *Educational Communication and Technology Journal, 33*(4), 249–262.

Clark, R. E. (1983). Reconsidering research on learning from media. *Review of Educational Research, 53*(4), 455–459.

Computer Curriculum Corporation. (1983). *Microhost instructional system.* Palo Alto, CA: Author.

Cognitronics Corporation. (1985). *Autoscor* [Computer Program]. Stamford, CT: Author.

Cooley, W. W., & Leinhardt, G. (1978). The instructional dimensions study: The search for effective classroom processes (Final report). Pittsburgh: University of Pittsburgh, Learning Research and Development Center. (ERIC Document No. ED 167 580)

Cohen, V. B. (1983). Criteria for the evaluation of microcomputer courseware. *Educational Technology, 23*(1), 9–14.

Cooper, A. (1980). Computer based learning at the Open University and the Cicero System, in R. Lewis, & E. D. Tagg (Eds.), *Computer assisted learning: Scope, progress, and limits.* Amsterdam: North-Holland.

Crawford, J., Evertson, C. M., Anderson, L. M., & Brophy, J. E. (1976). Process-product relationships in second and third grade classrooms. Austin, TX: The University of Texas, Research and Development Center for Teacher Education. (ERIC Document Reproduction Service No. ED 148 888)

Cruickshank, W., Bentzen, F., Ratzeburg, F., & Tannhauser, M. (1961). *A teaching method for brain-injured and hyperactive children.* Syracuse: Syracuse University Press.

DeCecco, J. P. (1968). *The psychology of learning and instruction: Educational psychology*. Englewood Cliffs, NJ: Prentice-Hall.

Deshler, D., Warner, M. M., Schumaker, J. B., & Alley, G. R. (1983). The learning strategies intervention model: Key components and current status. In J. D. McKinney, & L. Feagans (Eds.), *Current topics in learning disabilities* (Vol. 1). Norwood, NJ: Ablex.

Duffy, T. M., & Waller, R. (Eds.). (1985). *Designing usable texts*. New York: Academic Press.

Dunkleberger, G., & Knight, C. (1977). The influence of computer-managed self-paced instruction in science attitudes of students. *Journal of Research in Science Teaching, 14:* 551–555.

Durham County (NC) Public Schools (1986). Final report: The North Carolina consortium for microcomputer research with the handicapped. Durham, NC: Author.

Dynacomp, Inc. (1984). *The teacher's gradebook* [Computer Program]. Rochester, NY: Author.

Eggert, W. (1978, March). Teacher process variables and pupil products. Paper presented at the annual meeting of the American Educational Research Association, Toronto. (ERIC Document Reproduction Service No. ED 166 174)

Eisle, J. A. (1985). Computer-based authoring systems. In D. H. Hibasseb (Ed.), *The technology of text: Principles for structuring, designing, and displaying text* (2nd ed.), pp. 310–324. Englewood Cliffs, NJ: Educational Technology Publications.

Electronic Arts (1983). *Music construction set* [Computer Program]. Author.

Electronic Learning (1986). The Networked-Micro ILS, *5*(5), 44–47.

Emmer, E. T. (1981). Effective managment in junior high mathematics classrooms. Austin, TX: University of Texas, Research and Development Center for Teacher Education. (R & D Report No. 6111)

Emmer, E. T., Evertson, C. M., & Anderson, L. M. (1980). Effective classroom management at the beginning of the school year. *Elementary School Journal, 80,* 219–231.

Emmer, E. T., Sanford, J. P., Clements, B. S., & Martin, J. (1982). Improving classroom management and organization in junior high schools: An experimental investigation. Austin, TX: University of Texas, Research and Development Center for Teacher Education. (R & D Report No. 6153)

Emmer, E. T., Sanford, J. P., Evertson, C. M., Clements, B. S., & Martin, J. (1981). The classroom management improvement study: An experiment in elementary schools. Austin, TX: University of Texas, Research and Development Center for Teacher Education. (R & D Report No. 6050)

Evans, W., & Guyman, R. E. (1978, March). *Clarity of explanation: A powerful indicator of teacher effectiveness*. Paper presented at the annual meeting of the American Education Research Association, Toronto. (ERIC Document Reproduction Service No. ED 151 321)

Evertson, C. M., Anderson, L. M., & Brophy, J. E. (1978). *Process-outcome relationships in the Texas junior high school study: Compendium*. Washington:

National Institute of Education. (ERIC Document Reproduction Service No. ED 166 192)

Fisher, C. W., Filby, N. M., Marliave, R., Cahen, L. S., Dishaw, N. M., Moore, J. E., & Berliner, D. C. (1978). Teaching behaviors, academic learning time and student achievement: Final report of phase III-B. *Beginning Teachers Evaluation Study* (Technical report V-1). San Francisco, CA: Far West Laboratory for Educational Research and Development. (ERIC Document Reproduction Service No. 183 525)

Fisher, C. W., Filby, N. M., Marliave, R., Cahen, L. S., Dishaw, N. M., Moore, J. E., & Berliner, D. C. (1980). Teaching behaviors, academic learning time, and student achievement: An overview. In C. Denham, & A. Liebman (Eds.), *Time to learn*. Washington, DC: U.S. Government Printing Office.

Fortune, J. C. (1967). A study of the generality of presenting behavior in teaching. Memphis, TN: Memphis State University. (ERIC Document Reproduction Service No. ED 016 285)

Gage, N. L., Belgard, M., Dell, D., Hiller, J. E., Rosenshine, B., & Unruh, W. P. (1968). *Explorations of the teacher's effectiveness in explaining* (Technial report No. 4). Stanford, CA: Stanford University, Center for Educational Research. (ERIC Document Reproduction Service No. ED 028 147)

Gagne, R. M. (1985). *The conditions of learning and theory of instruction* (4th ed.). New York: Holt, Rinehart & Winston.

Gagne, R. M., Briggs, L. J., & Wager, W. W. (1988). *Principles of instructional design* (3rd ed.). New York: Holt, Rinehart & Winston.

Gay, L. R. (1985). *Educational evaluation and measurement: Competencies for analysis and application* (2nd ed.). Columbus, OH: Merrill.

Gersten, R. M., Carmine, D. W., & Williams, P. B. (1982). Measuring implementation of a structural educational model in an urban school district: An observational approach. *Educational Evaluation and Policy Analysis, 4,* 67–79.

Glaser, R. (1962). Psychology and instructional technology. In R. Glaser, *Training research and education*. Pittsburgh: University of Pittsburgh Press.

Goetz, E. T., & Armbruster, B. B. (1980). Psychological correlates of text structure. In R. J. Spiro, B. C. Bruce, & W. F. Bowers (Eds.), *Theoretical issues in reading comprehension: Prospectives from cognitive psychology, artificial intelligence, linguistics, and education*. Hillsdale, NJ: Erlbaum.

Good, T. L., & Brophy, J. E. (1984). *Looking in classrooms*. New York: Harper & Row.

Good, T. L., & Grouws, D. A. (1979). The Missouri mathematics effectiveness project: An experimental study in fourth grade classrooms. *Journal of Educational Psychology, 71,* 355–362.

Grimm, B., & Miller, S. (1985). *Word talk: Revolutionary talking word processing program* [Computer Program]. Fort Wayne, IN: Computer Aids Corporation.

Grobe, R. P., & Pettibone, T. J. (1975). Effect of instructional pace on student attentiveness. *The Journal of Educational Research, 69,* 131–134.

Group for the Study of Effective Teaching. (1983). Teaching Effectiveness Evaluation Project: Final report. Quality Assurance Program, State of North Carolina.

Hannum, W. H. (1986). Techniques for creating computer-based instructional text: Programming languages, authoring languages, and authoring systems. *Educational Psychologist, 21*(4), 293–314.

Hannum, W. H. (1988). Designing Courseware to Fit Subject Matter Structure. In D. H. Jonassen (Ed.), *Instructional designs for microcomputer courseware*. Hillsdale, NJ: Erlbaum.

Harmon, P., & King, D. (1985). *Expert systems: Artificial intelligence in business*. New York: Wiley.

Hartley Courseware, Inc. (1982). *E-Z PILOT* [Computer Program]. Dimondale, MI: Author.

Hartley, J. R., & Lovell, P. (1984). The psychological principles underlying the design of computer-based instructional systems. In D. Walker, & R. Hess, (Eds.), *Instructional software: Principles and perspectives for design and use*. Belmont, CA: Wadsworth.

Hasselbring, T., & Crossland, C. (1982). Application of microcomputer technology to spelling assessment of learning disabled students. *Learning Disability Quarterly, 5*, 80–82.

Heikkinen, H., & Dunkelberger, G. E. (1985, October 27–28). On disk with mastery learning. *The Science Teacher*.

Helsel-Dewert, M., & Vandenmeiracker, M. (1987). The intelligibility of synthetic speech to learning handicapped children. *Journal of Special Education Technology, 9*(1), 38–44.

Hiller, J. W., Fisher, G. A., & Kaess, W. (1969). A computer investigation of verbal characteristics of effective classroom lecturing. *American Educational Research Journal, 6*, 661–675.

Hirschbuhl, J. J. (1980). Hardware of considerations for computer based education in the 1980s. *Journal of Research and Development in Education, 14*(1), 41–46.

Hofmeister, A. (1984). *Microcomputer applications in the classroom*. New York: Holt, Rinehart & Winston.

Holt, Rinehart & Winston. (1984). Class II (Reading). New York: Author.

Houghton Mifflin. (1985). *The dolphin system*. Hanover, NH: Author.

Hughes, D. C. (1973). An experimental investigation of the effects of pupil responding and teacher reacting on pupil achievement. *American Educational Research Journal, 10*, 21–37.

Human, J., & Cohen, A. (1979). Learning mastery: Ten conclusions after 15 years and 3000 schools. *Educational Leadership, 37*, 104–106.

International Business Machines. (1985). *PILOT* [Computer Program]. Irving, TX: Author.

Jonassen, D. H. (Ed.) (1982). *The technology of text: Principles for structuring, designing, and displaying text*. Englewood Cliffs, NJ: Educational Technology Publications.

Jonassen, D. H. (Ed.). (1985). *The technology of text: Principles for structuring, designing, and displaying text* (2nd ed.). Englewood Cliffs, NJ: Educational Technology Publications.

Kearsley, G. (1982). *Costs, benefits, and productivity in training systems*. Reading, MA: Addison-Wesley.

Killian, C. R. (1983). Standardized testing and computer technology: New opportunities for improvement. *Educational Technology,* pp. 30–31.

Kirk, S. A., & Gallagher, J. J. (1986). *Educating exceptional children* (5th ed.). Boston: Houghton Mifflin.

Kounin, J. S. (1970). *Discipline and group management in classrooms.* Huntington, NY: Robert Krieger Publishing.

Kounin, J. S., Friesen, W. V., & Norton, A. E. (1966). Managing emotionally disturbed children in regular classrooms. *Journal of Educational Psychology, 57,* 1–13.

Kozma, R. (1982). Instructional design in a chemistry laboratory course: The impacts of structure and aptitudes on performance and attitudes. *Journal of Research in Science Teaching, 19,* 261–270.

Krug, S. E. (1987). *Psychware sourcebook.* Kansas City: Test Corportion of America.

Krupski, A. (1985). Variations in attention as a function of classroom task demands in learning handicapped and CA-matched non-handicapped children. *Exceptional Children, 52*(1), 52–56.

Kulik, J. A., Bangert, R. L., & Williams, G. W. (1983). Effects of computer-based teaching on secondary school students. *Journal of Educational Psychology, 75*(1), 19–26.

Laddaga, R., Levine, A., & Suppes, P. (1977). *Research on uses of audio and natural language processing in CAI: Third year report.* (Tech sciences.) Stanford, CA: Stanford University.

Land, M. L., & Smith, L. R. (1979). Effect of a teacher clarify variable on student achievement. *Journal of Educational Research, 72,* 196–198.

Leinhardt, G. (1977, April). *Applying a classroom process model to instructional evaluation.* Paper presented at the annual meeting of the American Educational Research Association, New York. (ERIC Document Reproduction Service No. ED 150 197)

Lillie, D. L., & Edwards, E. D. (1986a). *Instructional management system* [Unpublished Computer Program]. Chapel Hill, NC.

Lillie, D., L., & Edwards, E. D. (1986b). *Unistar II+*: Computer-assisted Pre IEP Program. East Aurora, NY: Slosson Educational Publications.

Lillie, D. L., & Edwards, E. D. (1987). A generic computer-based error analysis program [Unpublished software program]. Chapel Hill: NC.

Lindsey, J. D. (1987). *Computers and exceptional individuals.* Columbus, OH: Merrill.

Macmillan Company (1985). *SERIES r Instructional Management System* [Computer Program]. New York: Author.

Martin, J., Veldman, D. J., & Anderson, L. M. (1980). Within-class relationships between student achievement and teacher behaviors. *American Educational Research Journal, 17,* 479–490.

McConnell, J. W. (1977, April). *Relationships between selected teacher behaviors and attitudes/achievement of algebra classes.* Paper presented at the annual meeting of the American Educational Research Association, New York. (ERIC Document Reproduction Service No. ED 141 118)

McCune, S. (1982). Restructuring essential for American education. *State Education Leader, 1*(4), 3–5.

McDonald, F. J. (1976). Report on phase II of the Beginning Teacher Evaluation Study. *Journal of Teacher Education, 27*(1), 39–42.

Mercer, C. D. (1987). *Students with Learning Disabilities* (3rd ed.). Columbus, OH: Merrill.

Mercer, C. D., & Mercer, A. R. (1985). *Teaching Students with Learning Problems* (2nd ed.). Columbus, OH: Merrill.

Merrill, M. D. (1985). Where is the authoring in authoring systems? *Journal of Computer-Based Instruction, 12*(4), 90–96.

Merrill, M. D., Schneider, E. W., & Fletcher, K. A. (1980). *TICCIT*. Englewood Cliffs, NJ: Educational Technology Publications.

Micropi (1985). *MacPILOT* [Computer Program]. Bellingham, WA: Author.

Millman, J., & Arter, J. A. (1984). Issues in item banking. *Journal of Educational Measures, 21*(4), 315–330.

Omotayo, O. R. (1983). A microcomputer-based reading aid for blind students. *IEEE Transactions on Education, E-26*(4), 156–161.

O'Shea, T., & Self, J. (1983). *Learning and teaching with computers: Artificial intelligence in education.* Englewood Cliffs, NJ: Prentice-Hall.

Pace, A. J. (1985). Learning to learn through text design: Can it be done? In D. H. Jonassen (Ed.), *The technology of text: Principles for structuring, designing, and displaying text* (2nd ed.). Englewood Cliffs, NJ: Educational Technology Publications.

Papert, S. (1980). *Mindstorms: Children, computers and powerful ideas.* New York: Basic Books.

Pea, R. D., & Kurland, D. M. (1984). On the cognitive effects of learning computer-programming. *New Idea PS, 2*(2), 137–168.

Reigeluth, C. M., & Stein, F. S. (1983). The elaboration theory of instruction. In C. M. Reigeluth (Ed.), *Instructional design theories and models: An overview of their current status.* Hillsdale, NJ: Erlbaum.

Reinhold, F. (1986). Bringing technology to special education in the bayou state. *Electronic learning, 6*(1), 38–40.

Rich, E. (1983). *Artificial intelligence.* New York: McGraw-Hill.

Rowe, M. B. (1974). Wait-time and rewards as instructional variables: Their influence on language, logic, and fate control. Part I: Wait-time. *Journal of Research in Science Teaching, 11*, 81–94.

Rushakoff, G. E., & Bull, G. L. (1986). Microcomputers in communication disorders. *Computers in the Schools, 3*(3/4), 141–157.

Rushakoff, G. E., & Edwards, W. (1982). The /s/ meter: A beginning for microcomputer assisted articulation therapy. Paper presented at the American Speech-Language-Hearing Association annual convention, Toronto.

Rhyne, J. M. (1982). Comprehension of synthetic speech by blind children. *Journal of Visual Impairment and Blindness, 76*, 313–316.

School District of Pittsburgh (1985). A guide to the MAP program. Pittsburgh: Author.

Science Research Associates (1985). *Micro Test Administration system* [Computer Program]. Chicago: Author.

Senf, G. M. (1983). Learning disabilities challenge courseware. *The Computing Teacher, 2*, 18–19.

Sension, D. (1985, February). Test programs help teachers boost learning, *School Tech News*.

Smith, L. R. (1977). Aspects of teacher discourse and student achievment in mathematics. *Journal for Research in Mathematics Education, 8*, 195–204.

Smith, L. R., & Cotten, M. L. (1980). Effect of lesson vagueness and discontinuity on student achievement and attitudes. *Journal of Educational Psychology, 72*, 670–675.

Smith, L. R., & Edmonds, E. M. (1978). Teacher vagueness and pupil participation in mathematics learning. *Journal for Research in Mathematics Education, 9*, 228–232.

Stallings, J. A. (1978, March). Teaching basic reading skills in secondary schools. Paper presented at the annual meeting of the American Educational Research Association, Toronto. (ERIC Document Reproduction Service No. ED 166 634)

Stanford Center for Research and Development. (1975). Preliminary report of a factorially designed experiment on teacher structuring, soliciting, and reacting. Stanford, CA: Stanford University, Center for Research and Development in Teaching. (ERIC Document Reproduction Service No. ED 113 329)

Suppes, P. (1984). Observations about the application of artificial intelligence research to education. In D. Walker, & R. Hess (Eds.), *Instructional software: Principles and perspectives for design and use*. Belmont, CA: Wadsworth.

Taylor, R. (Ed.) (1980). *The computer in the school: Tutor, tool, tutee*. New York: Teachers College Press.

Tennyson, R. D., & Park, O. C. (1980). *The teaching of concepts: A review of instructional design research literature*. Review of Educational Research, 50, 55–70.

Toffler, A. (1980). *The Third Wave*. New York: Morrow.

Torgesen, J. K. (1986). Using computers to help learning disabled children practice reading: A research-based perspective. *Learning Disabilities Focus, 1*(2), 72–81.

Torgesen, J. K., & Young, K. (1983). Priorities for the use of microcomputers with learning disabled children. *Journal of Learning Disabilities, 16*, 234–237.

Unisys Corporation (1987a). *The ICON system*. Detroit: Author.

Unisys Corporation (1987b). *MicroCASTs computer managed instruction system*. Detroit: Author.

Unisys/UNC-CH Technology Project (1987). Final Report, 1986–1987. University of North Carolina at Chapel Hill, School of Education.

U.S. Department of Education (1986). *What works: Research about teaching and learning*. Washington, DC: Author.

Vacc, H. N. (1987). Word processor versus handwriting: A comparative study of writing samples produced by mildly handicapped students. *Exceptional Children, 54*(2), 156–165.

Vasu, E. S., & Vasu, M. L. (1987). Integrating computers into social science curricula: Computer literacy and beyond. *Social Science Microcomputer Review, 3*(1), 1985.

Wang, M. C., Rubenstein, J. L., & Reynolds, M. C. (1985). Clearing the road to success for students with special needs. *Educational Leadership*, pp. 62–67.

Webb, N. M. (1982). Group composition, group interaction, and achievement in cooperative small groups. *Journal of Educational Psychology, 74*, 475–484.

Wicat Systems. (1984). Wicat system 300. Minneapolis, MN: Author.

Winne, P. H., & Marx, R. W. (1982). Students' and teachers' views of thinking processes for classroom learning. *Elementary School Journal, 82*, 493–518.

Wolfolk, A. E. (1987). *Educational psychology* (3rd ed.). Englewood Cliffs, NJ: Prentice-Hall.

Woodcock, R. (1978). Woodcock-Johnson psycho-educational battery. Hingham, MA: DLM-Teaching Resources Corporation.

Wright, C. J., & Nuthall, G. (1970). Relationships between teacher behaviors and pupil achievement in three experimental elementary science lessons. *American Educational Research Journal, 7*, 477–491.

Xerox Corporation (1986). *Ventura Publisher*. Rochester, NY: Author.

Index